GARDEN
of Blu

MISTI BLU DAY MCDERMOTT

IMAGINEWE
Publishers

ImagineWe Publishers
New York Florida South Carolina

Cover Illustration/Art by Angela Emr
Cover Design and Photo by Stephanie Spoly &
Keith Knauer of CosmicCapture

Published by ImagineWe, LLC
ImagineWe Publishers
247 Market Street, Suite 201
Lockport, NY 14094
United States
imaginewellc.com

ISBN: 978-1-946512-44-4
Library of Congress Control Number: 2021914871

First Edition

The National Suicide Prevention Lifeline is 1-800-273-8255

This memoir reflects the author's life, rendered to the best of her ability.

**Check out her website &
follow her on social media!**

mistibludream.com
bludreamhealth.com
@mistibluday

DEDICATION

To anyone I may have hurt throughout my process of healing. To my husband, children, extended family, and close friends: thank you for loving me. To those who are lost and wandering: may you find your way through the dark.

To my dad, my grandmothers, my cousin Brandon, my beautiful friend Red, and everyone else who left us here on Earth to become our angels.

Contents

FOREWORD

Astrid Phillips
(Misti's Daughter)

Resilience to me means to cope in a healthy way after going through something harsh. Growing up, I saw my mom deal with multiple things at once, like chronic illnesses and being able to manage them along with work and school.

I hope my generation can find healthy coping mechanisms that help with their struggles. I also hope my generation takes the time to work on themselves, grow, and heal in a positive way. You're not alone. Having someone to talk to is very important and normal. Keeping yourself busy or having healthy coping mechanisms helps.

PREFACE

This book takes you through the painful stages of growth, chews you up, and spits you out into a world that makes a little more sense and shines a little brighter. Navigating life is a difficult feat, as many of us spend a portion of life mending the wounds of trauma.

I know my traumas have traumatized others, spilling over into a cyclical mess that inevitably continued to grow like an invasive vine. Our traumas are unrelenting, affecting others when we don't learn how to manage and cope. I spent far too much time feeling incapacitated and endlessly wandering without a plan. I was aimlessly surviving. It takes just the smallest poke to spill over. I was often seeking validation and filling a void. I was lonely, yet now I realize that healed people are not lonely when they are content with themselves.

Many of us only want guidance when it is in our favor. It isn't until you are open to accept change, take risks, and to put in the effort when you can make the shift you need to better yourself. It starts with a seedling of courage that tickles your throat, waiting to bloom into a voice.

You deserve nothing but the best in life. You deserve to be seen and heard. You deserve the love, care and respect that you give to others. When you are a warrior, remember that scars grow back stronger. Healing is ugly, but it's brave. It's painful, but it's powerful. It's messy, but it's worth it.

Before you can heal, you must first acknowledge what is broken. You cannot heal from something you refuse to see. The biggest leap you can take is recognizing what you have been denying all along.

Fuck fear. The unknown is just an adventure. You can let it burn your world down or set ablaze a new path.

ONE

Golden Rose

"Golden rose, the color of a dream I had
Not too long ago
A misty blue and the lilac too
A never to grow old"
-One Rainy Wish by Jimi Hendrix

I t's 1984 and the sun is warm enough to blanket your skin, keeping you comfortable from the cool breeze. We're in Riverside, California and it's August 21st, a Tuesday morning. Ronald Reagan is the president and Ray Parker Jr.'s Ghostbusters is the number one song, while previously it was When Doves Cry by Prince. It was ten days after my expected due date and even still, I didn't turn my body around to prepare for my entrance into the world. Instead, I was being evacuated from my mother's womb because I was 8 pounds, 11 ounces and my time was up. My dad started his yellow truck and my mom hopped in. As they drove to Riverside General Hospital, my dad anxiously tapped his thumbs on the steering wheel to the beat of the song on the radio.

My mom had a cesarean delivery since I was breech. She recalls seeing my chest flutter since I was a baby. My arrhythmias and fast heart rates were impossible to catch and I was seemingly healthy. During my first year of life, we lived with our windows boarded up. Richard Ramirez, known as the "Night Stalker" and the "Valley Intruder," was prowling the Greater Los Angeles area.

I had a recurring dream for many years growing up. *In the dream, I was under a year old and couldn't walk yet. I was alone, sitting in the grass in our front yard. My dad had gone inside to make a phone call. I looked around and could see the front of our house and then to the left, a truck pulled over. A man quickly hopped out of the truck and walked over towards me, reaching to pick me up. Then my dad runs out of the house, yelling at the strange man.* I always wonder if that dream was actually a memory, tucked away.

For those who have experienced trauma, memory loss can be a natural survival skill and a way to protect oneself from psychological damage. Dissociative amnesia allows a person to cope with a traumatic event. Looking back, much of my life has missing pieces. It's as if some of the pages were torn out. I know deep down that there is something I am keeping from myself. My brain has suppressed memories, yet I still have plenty of other vivid ones to recall.

I survived earthquakes in California, tornados in Missouri, and hurricanes in Florida. I survived open-heart surgery, heart break, loss, trauma, and cancer. Just when I think I am okay and on steady ground, something knocks me on my ass again. It couldn't all be for nothing. The battles I have fought have meaning. I couldn't suppress my voice and carry the heaviness alone anymore. I found the urge to share my vulnerability in order to lead others through their brokenness. I felt so alone, yet looking back I realize I was alone because I built a wall. No one could see through my fortress, as many of us are conditioned to hide pain.

TWO

Yoo-hoo and Lunchables

*"Though I try to talk sense to myself,
But I just won't listen."*
-Oh Well by Fiona Apple

I had a boyfriend in preschool. Yeah, I know...it was preschool! But he was my boyfriend and we were in love, or whatever that means for a young child. He came to my birthday party at a McDonalds somewhere in California. He got me an orange lunchbox with a zebra on it and a Barbie with a Barbie car. They were the best gifts I received from anyone. I remember his birthday party and how big his yard was, with the greenest grass and a huge, beautiful home. At his party there were several electric cars, so no one had to take turns. I remember riding in the electric car with him, laughing while the wind blew through my hair on a beautiful sunny day. During play time in preschool we would kiss and pretend to be superheroes on the playground. When I was told we would be moving to Portland, Oregon, I was so devastated to say goodbye.

GARDEN OF BLU

It was my last time coming to that preschool class before we would be moving far away. When I arrived to grab my things and say goodbye, I searched for him so that I could cry and hug him. There he was. My eyes lit up for a brief moment until I realized he was holding my friend's hand, another little girl who seemed to have replaced me. I teared up and turned around, with no intention of saying goodbye to them. I felt so betrayed, meaningless, and replaceable.

It was time to start over again. I remember snow and rainy days. My half-sister had come to visit and she was my idol. I looked up to her and it was not often when I would get to see her. We only lived in Portland, Oregon for a little under a year before we moved back to California. My parents were not fans of the gloomy weather. We then moved to Paradise, California where our answering machine played, "Take me down to the paradise city where the grass is green and the girls are pretty," by Guns N' Roses.

One of my favorite memories in Paradise was climbing up into a tree in front of our house. I would hide and read. I would daydream. My dad was a building inspector and worked in construction. My mom suggested that we move to Branson, Missouri, as it was newly built and had a lot of potential work for him. I told my friends, who had skin tones in every shade, that I was moving to Missouri.

"Where is that?" they asked.

"I don't know," I said, puzzled. I just knew it was far away from the ocean.

I was excited to go somewhere new, but sad to leave my friends. We moved every year and sometimes in the middle of the school year. I was always painfully shy, and when I finally made friends it was time to leave again. This time, it was the farthest I had been. It turns out that Clever, Missouri was a little town in the middle of the country. The population was a little over 500 residents, with one officer and a small market with video tape rentals. It was a culture shock. Palm trees had turned into oak and elm trees. People talked differently and everyone had the same skin tone.

I walked into my third grade class, being introduced at the front of the room as every kid stared at me. My heart was racing and I could feel the heat of my face turning red. *Please don't make me talk*, I thought.

"Why don't you introduce yourself?" said the teacher.

I felt like I would die before I could get a sound out that resembled my name. "I'm Misti," I muttered while staring at the floor. "Her name is Misti Blu Day!" The teacher said out loud as everyone snickered. A girl with big red hair, freckles and perfect teeth hopped over to me and grabbed my arm, "I'll show you around! My name's Big Red, like the bubblegum." I instantly felt safe and I had a new friend.

We lived on a few acres of land and someone was paying my dad to let their cows roam the field next to our house. One night, my dad ran out of the house after seeing a cow running loose. We lived off of State Highway 14. My mom walked outside to help, followed by my brother and his curiosity. My entire family was outside, in the dark, chasing a cow near a highway. Suddenly, the driver of a semi truck slammed on the brakes. I heard a loud sound followed by tires screeching. My family was nowhere to be seen, but I could make out something on the road. I screamed and fell to the ground. My nine year old brain comprehended that my entire family was just run over by a semi truck. The truck actually hit the cow and my family was safe, but I will never forget how crippled with fear I felt.

Growing up, I was a terrible student. I had a very difficult time focusing and my head was always in the clouds. I never thrived in a classroom setting. I would stare at the posters on the classroom walls or draw in my notebook. I remember giving my arm hickeys in the first grade and telling my teacher I had a rash so that I could be sent home. Another time, I was running in gym class and my heart was racing. Being hypermobile and knowing it was a bizarre feature I had, I twisted my arm around 360 degrees and ran to the coach, showing them my fake sprained arm. They were horrified, but since I had a stoic look on my face they knew it was bullshit. They were very confused and puzzled as to how my arm could look so strange. I took off and got back to running laps while my heart fluttered.

Junior high and high school were worse. We moved to a nearby town called Nixa. In junior high, my face would turn bright red from my heart racing in the 250-300s. My skin was clammy and gym was always my last class before riding the bus home. I was too exhausted to change back into my regular clothes and planned to shower once I got home, so I didn't bother changing out of my gym clothes. One day, I walked down the skinny aisle of the bus and everyone was staring at me. They were laughing and whispering. I tried to ignore it and pretend that I wasn't mortified and angry. *As if I didn't have enough shit to deal with*, I thought. I was constantly teased for being the last girl in school to develop breasts. I still didn't have my period and didn't until I was 15. My dad was an alcoholic so my home life wasn't exactly at its best. This was also the age where depression was at an entirely new level, yet mental health was not yet recognized.

YOO-HOO & LUNCHABLES

Just as I sat down and the bus took off, everyone stood up to get a good view of what transpired next. A girl who lived down the street, started walking towards me, smiling so big she couldn't contain herself. She handed me a gift and laughed. The gift bag looked thoughtful and well put together. Of course my mind didn't process that this was going to be a gift from malice and not something sweet, even though I was not friends with this girl. For a split second, the birthday-like gift bag felt like a nice peace offering. As I unwrapped the colorful tissue paper, I saw Suave shampoo, soap, and a stack of pads for the period I didn't have. The entire bus burst into laughter as my blood boiled from the emotional burn I just felt. I stood up and stomped over to her, throwing the bag into her lap. I wanted to hurt her in every way that she hurt me, but the words I spewed out of anger only made me look more foolish.

In high school, I finally had breasts. I didn't have to be shy in the locker room while other girls said, "Wow, you are as flat as the wall!" All of my friends already had boyfriends, and for once, maybe I would too. I was still incredibly shy and didn't really have a group of people that I fit in with. I was too much of a prude for the goth kids because I didn't drink or smoke. I wasn't stylish enough for the preppy kids and my worn clothes showed that I didn't come from money. My grades weren't good enough to hang out with the smart kids. I think I fell somewhere into the artsy misfits clique.

Many people told me later in life that I was very aloof and intimidating. In high school, my depression was in full bloom and would continue to grow for the next decade. I never acknowledged mental health and it was never a normalized topic at that time. Back then, if you saw a therapist then you had major problems. It was not as accepted then to see a therapist as it is today.

Most of the time, when I met a new female friend, it was because she had a crush on my brother. She would ask if she could stay the night and I would end up watching tv by myself. My life was shaping me to not trust people. I didn't trust anyone's intentions. The few friends I had were very close friends. When I trusted someone, I felt like I could be my genuine self, unfiltered and weird.

I always loved solitude and still do; solitude is how I recharge. Even when I was younger, I needed time alone. I needed breaks. Since skipping school was part of my routine, it was therapeutic to just stay at home alone while everyone was off to work or school. The sun shined brighter on those days and I felt at peace. In high school, my grades were Ds and Fs, with the occasional C. My lowest GPA one semester was 1.49. I didn't care. Not only did I not care but I also had no idea or guidance on what my plans were after high school. It didn't even matter to me.

When I moved to Florida in the middle of my junior year, I made it through that semester. I missed a few days and went home early or came in late. It wasn't enough to raise any red flags. The second half of my junior year was adjusting from being the new kid again. I came from Missouri where fashion was important. Most of the girls stole clothes so that they could have new outfits. Gadzooks was my favorite store. I was in the dressing room with a friend in Missouri and she didn't take off the shirt she tried on. Instead, she put her sweater on over her shirt and stuffed her bra with a swimsuit. She stuffed a shirt in my purse and said, "Let's go." I was in shock. I was so frozen by fear that I just went with it, heart racing and all. I felt like I would pass out before we reached the exit. "Act cool," she said as we bolted.

Florida was so different. Everyone was more casual. Guys wore board shorts. Girls wore sandals and tank tops. Everyone looked like they came from the beach or were headed to the beach after class. There I was, the new girl with the weird name, dressed in Bubblegum red pleather pants with strappy platform sandals, a tight black top, and a black ribbon worn as a choker.

"What are you?" a girl asked, confused as to where I belonged.

"Huh?" I questioned.

"Like, I can't figure you out. You're, like, too pretty to be grunge but too weird to be preppy. You're sort of artsy, but some days punk or goth, but then you wear dresses or preppy jeans other days. I don't get it."

I didn't know where I fit in either. I usually gravitated to the other misfits, the ones with mohawks or green hair. I never understood why people hung out with just one clique of people. I liked people for who they were, despite their hair color or brand of clothes. Somehow it felt like I had to choose which flock of birds my feathers matched.

Halfway through my senior year, I was called to the office. The guidance counselor told me that I was failing due to absences. I questioned that statement, as I actually had better grades that year. I had started to look into going to the Art Institute of Fort Lauderdale for photography, or to the University of Rochester Medicine Sleep Center to study sleep disorders. I was fascinated with sleep disorders after experiencing sleep paralysis at the age of fifteen. I spent time trying to skate by so that I could graduate and maybe go to college. I even went to summer school to make up for previous F's. I was on track to graduate after finishing this last semester and here this woman was telling me I had to stop going to school and come back next year, because this semester wouldn't count. Florida had a nine day rule. If you racked up more than nine unexcused absences in a semester, you would fail. Somehow I missed this memo.

There I was, seventeen with one semester left and I had to repeat a semester and come back next year. Staying home once a week was how I survived the other 4 days. It was how I was able to thrive and raise my grades and pass. I felt defeated, but also I felt like my school didn't care about where I ended up. I drove home in the middle of the afternoon. I was now a high school dropout.

Shortly after leaving my high school, just before prom and graduation, I enrolled in the adult education program to get my GED. I did a practice exam and passed, so I signed up for the real deal. I had my high school GED before I would have earned my diploma. I was invited to prom with friends but I felt embarrassed. I didn't want to celebrate anyone's graduation because I was left behind and I felt robbed. It hurt too much to face what I missed out on.

I lost a lot of friends at a young age, many friends from Missouri. My first friend in Clever was in a fatal car accident. In high school, several others were in fatal car accidents. To this day, Nixa has a Facebook group to honor the many friends we have lost over the years. My cousin is one of them. Living in Florida so long at this point, I can say I have lost just as many friends here, mostly to drugs. I often wonder why my generation seems to lose so many young people so soon.

THREE

Lake of Fire

"You can run on for a long time
Sooner or later,
God'll cut you down."
-God's Gonna Cut You Down by Johnny Cash

Growing up, I went through several religious phases. Part of Alcoholics Anonymous includes God, or at least for my dad it did. My dad would turn to church when he struggled with sobriety. One of the first churches I remember going to in the early 90s, was an evangelistic biker church in Anaheim, California. The parking lot was full of motorcycles and people wore whatever they wanted. In Missouri, we went to a Baptist church. The Sunday lessons included stringing yarn through dried macaroni noodles as we listened to stories about heaven and hell. Hell was so intriguing and terrifying. At a young age, I visually imagined a lake of fire where people burned for all of eternity for their sins. I was traumatized by the mere thought of being separated from my family and loved ones. How could I enjoy heaven while they were burning in hell simply because they didn't invite Jesus into their hearts?

I wondered, *what if someone sins and then dies before they can ask God for forgiveness?* As soon as I got home, I wrote my sister a letter to ask if she let Christ in her heart. She had to be saved! Who else could I save?

1993

Dear Summer,
You have to get baptised are else you won't go to heaven. You also have to stop sinning and you could go to heaven. I miss you very much. Visit us soon. Katie and Foxie are fine. Oh and PLEASE GET BAPTISED. I go to Girl Scouts and I get to sell cookies. Well see yah soon.
LOVE
MISTI

By Sis

❋ ❋ ❋

One of the church members that was very high up in the community reminded me of Ned Flanders from the Simpsons. He was so gentle that he almost seemed meek. He couldn't hurt a fly and his voice was always high pitched. Something felt off with him, yet the church adored him. One evening outside, it was dark and I heard loud noises. Ned Flanders lived in the home behind ours. We shared a fence. I was sneaking around in the shadows to get a closer look. His voice didn't sound like the soft, gentle voice that I knew. He was slamming things around and yelling. He backhanded his wife. I couldn't understand who this person was. It was as if he were possessed. The next time I was at church, he was still the same gentleman as before. I felt angry as he sat next to his wife, pretending to be a loving husband. I knew this dark secret, a darkness that he hid well. I witnessed it and didn't understand how no one knew who he really was.

My dad wasn't much different. He had a very welcoming presence. He truly had the biggest, most generous heart. It was so full of love and his laugh was contagious. Some nights my dad's luminous soul would diminish. It would get so buried, drowned by alcohol and that charming laugh would fade into a broken wail. I had seen him raise his fist to the sky and curse God some days, while crying and praising God the next. Some days he tickled us and made breakfast, while other days he stumbled around looking for someone to take his hurt out on. I would often resent him when people told me how cool he was, or how sweet and handsome he was. *If they only knew, I thought.*

There were nights I would hide in my closet, trying to drown out the sound of him hitting and throwing my mom around. I would use the end of a lost plastic Barbie shoe to clean under my nails, one by one. I later realized that my mom would do this with my nails, just not with a Barbie shoe. It was a comfort thing. Still to this day, I fidget with my nails when I am anxious. My closet felt like a small, safe place. I would see things that I never noticed before, like dried flakes of Play-Doh, lost doll accessories that the vacuum missed, and coats that I barely wore. It was quieter but I could still make out the occasional door slam. My legs would shake with fear and I just wanted to curl up in the dark.

GARDEN OF BLU

In Missouri, my parents went to church less but I still wanted to go. A lot of people from school went and I was very involved at my church. It was a Pentecostal church in the Bible Belt. People would speak in tongues and even one sermon was about going to hell if you couldn't speak in tongues. I was surely going to hell because there was no way I could ever do that, as shy as I was. I went to church every Wednesday and Sunday. I think I went to church and prayed so frequently because I was adamant about getting my prayers answered. I wanted my dad to stop abusing my mom and brother, and I wanted my heart to be fixed. There was a Christian store in Nixa, Missouri. I would spend my allowance there. I bought expensive notebooks to take notes on each bible study. Once, I bought fake twenty-dollar bills that had God's message when you opened it up. I was in junior high and put these in people's lockers, hoping to save others. I was determined to be a good Christian girl and thought that maybe it would get my prayers answered. After asking someone at the church why my prayers were never answered, they told me it was because I didn't have enough faith.

There was a time during junior high when I was in a parking lot across from my house, near the plaza with the Christian store. Two boys from school came up on their bikes, circling around and around while I stood in the middle with a friend. I was being teased again about my flat chest. When he circled back around, I punched him. He flew off his bike, landed on his pager and broke it. I had become so sick of being teased that I became angry and sometimes violent. My brother and cousins loved Mortal Kombat, Jean-Claude Van Damm, and Jackie Chan, so fighting was natural for me.

LAKE OF FIRE

My best friend went to an Episcopal church, where for the first time I felt the warm, fuzzy feeling of wine going down my throat at communion. I was invited to her church lock-in. It was an exciting night because there were no parents, just a few adults that stayed upstairs. There were both girls and guys and we were all young teenagers. At one point, everyone was smoking cigarettes outside. When I was offered one, I said no. My friend said yes. I felt way out of my element. We went inside and one of the boys, the really cute one, was interested in me. I hadn't even kissed anyone yet and the thought of anything sexual scared me. I wasn't curious yet at that age, though I should have been. My friends were losing their virginity and I couldn't imagine doing the same. He was sitting next to me and leaned in to kiss me. I was exhilarated that he even found me interesting or pretty. I felt his lips on mine and as his tongue began to part my lips, I smiled and turned away while blushing. I wasn't ready to make out and everyone else was coupling up. I felt lucky that he wanted to kiss me, but I just couldn't. I don't think I even really knew what to do. Hoping he would understand and continue to get to know me, I was startled by a loud thud. He hit the wall next to me and walked out of the room. He wasn't going to get to first base with me so he was over it. I felt like his charm was all a show to try to see how far he would get with me. He moved on to someone else. I was feeling alone and nervous about what happened so I started to look for my friend. I peeked in a room and found a couple hooking up. "Oh my god, sorry!" I shut the door. Walking down the dark quiet hallways of the church, I wondered where my friend was. I felt very codependent at times in our friendship. I wasn't ready for her to grow up without me. *It was only 9:00 p.m. and I had to live through another 10 hours of this shit,* I thought. How would I survive? Each minute felt like hours. Why are the adults so oblivious, I wondered. I hated myself for being such a prude and I wished I could be anyone but myself. Why couldn't I just have fun like everyone else? Not too long after, the boy who was my sort-of-first-kiss was working on his vehicle. The vehicle rolled over him and took his life.

Around that time, my best friend's father passed away too. I remember we had a track meet that day. When she didn't show up at school, I was pissed. *I can't believe she ditched me and I have to go to this meet alone*, I anxiously thought. Suddenly, I saw my dad, who was holding back tears. *Why is my dad here?* The bus was about to start loading up for the meet and I was getting checked out of school. "Her dad passed away," he said as he hugged me. He took me over to her house so that I could be there for her. I could hear her cry from outside. I remember sitting on the floor of her room where the pink phone from the game Electronic Dream Phone sat nearby. One moment we were just young girls and suddenly it didn't feel like that anymore.

One Wednesday night during my freshman year of high school, I stood up at the front of the youth service like I did every week. A prayer partner would come up and pray with anyone who had the guts to come forward. A lot of kids from my school were dating, hooking up, and partying. I was doing my best to impress God so that my heart would heal and my dad would be sober. That night, no one came up to pray with me. I was sick of trying. I was sick of being a good Christian girl while everyone had fun, and I was sick of praying for something that would never get better. I walked out and never looked back.

I didn't step foot in a church again until years later. We had moved to Florida and my dad was sober for a short time. He found a church down the road and he was doing well. He begged and begged for me to come with him. I was 16 at the time and since I was new to Florida, I was open to making new friends. I agreed to meet the youth director at a local bookstore. I didn't have a car at the time so I was dropped off and the 24-year-old youth pastor offered to give me a ride home. I suddenly realized I was being set up with the youth pastor. I awkwardly got out of the car and thanked him for the ride. I had no intention of ever meeting him again.

Weeks later my dad begged me to come to a church service. It was a Sunday, a packed parking lot, but as much as I dreaded going it seemed very important to him. I was very shy growing up, or perhaps I had social anxiety. There was a moment when I was sitting next to my dad as he sang and tapped his foot to the beat of the worship song. He was glowing and for a moment, I felt happy for him. Suddenly, my name was called over the microphone. The pastor asked me to come up to the front of the church, in front of everyone. My heart sank into the pit of my stomach.

No. No fucking way.

The pressure of my dad and the entire church looking at me pushed me to walk to the front, instead of a dramatic exit to the nearest door. The pastor put his hand on my chest, praying in the microphone for my heart. "Please Jesus, our Lord and Savior, heal this young woman's heart! In the name of the Father, and of the Son, and of the Holy Spirit. Amen." Though I know his intentions were good, I felt betrayed. Everyone was hugging my dad, feeling sorry for him. "His poor daughter and her broken heart." I felt like a token for him to be showered in attention, though now as I look back, I know it was just his way of coping.

GARDEN OF BLU

My track record with religion built me to be closed off from anything involving a church. No one seemed real and nothing was what it seemed. It felt like a gimmick and a life of fear and playing pretend. If you did anything great, it was because of God, not your own hard work. If something bad happened, then it was for a reason that only God knew. Many people were blessed but so many others suffered; it didn't seem fair.

I have taken world religions in college and have been to Buddhist temples, and while I can appreciate the culture and beauty in different religions it is still something that I continue to heal from. I have slowly opened up to spirituality thanks to having a circle of beautiful shaman friends and watching their growth and beauty unfold from healing. On a recent Sunday afternoon, a few of us met in a park and sat under a beautiful tree. Everyone was so open, transparent, and nurturing. We lifted each other up. There was no judgment or shows to put on. It was just the four of us - strong women, who have been through some shit, sharing our healing and taking in the beauty of the universe. It was so beautiful, raw and real.

Religion showed me judgment and taught me that I wasn't worthy of my prayers being answered. I was a sinner and I'd never be enough. The way I see things now is that we are all healing from the moment we enter this world. I appreciate the ugliness in pain because it offers strength. I value heartache because it brings resilience. I admire the dark because it makes everything else much brighter.

FOUR

Brick Wall

"A modern day woman with a weak constitution,
'Cause I've got monsters still under my
bed that I could never fight off"
-Hope is a Dangerous Thing for a Woman Like Me to Have by Lana Del Rey

B rick by brick, I was slowly building a wall as I moved through life. This wall would grow stronger and taller with each year that passed. I became jaded after each relationship, I trusted no one, and I believed it was me against the world.

Brick 1

My father thought I was a lie. There was my mother, pregnant, and he was getting back into a previous relationship. He was through with us. He was tired of looking at my mother's bruised face and hopeful eyes. My brother was three at the time and I was a little egg fertilized by mistakes in a womb of disaster. If I was just a lie like he thought, I would have saved my mother and brother from the trauma ahead. But there I was, implanted in a whirlpool of love and hate, expected in August in a belly that brought everyone back together.

33

Brick 8

I remember the days we did chores and got a few bucks at the end of the week. I emptied the dishwasher and fed the cats, set the table--you know, the things little girls are trained to do in order to prepare to be a pregnant and barefoot housewife, cleaning her home, with dinner on the table. This means my brothers did the boy stuff like mowing the lawn, taking out the trash, and feeding the dogs. At the end of the week we'd get those few dollars that made it all worth it. My brothers would burn holes in their pockets while I saved every penny since the day I could count change. My eyes have always been clouded by hopes and dreams to buy my escape. It was my little secret, my way out, in that glass piggy bank on my dresser. Sometimes my piggy bank would get so full and I'd feel so proud and hopeful and then my father would empty it out, every penny, promising to pay it back one day. Sometimes my brothers grabbed a few quarters too.

He'd return later that night, stumbling in while drunk and belligerent, looking for my mother. I'd lock myself in my room, in my closet or under my bed and try to make sense of what was going on outside of my room. I knew. He had used my money, which were my hopes, to poison his mind with whiskey and then place his hurt into my mother's body. He emptied my hopes into his wallet for several years after that.

Brick 14

One Christmas, we were home after a family party at my grandmother's house where all of our cousins, aunts, and uncles ate and exchanged gifts. My grandmother's house was always packed and it was my favorite time of the year. Everyone was so happy and our entire family was together. It was our tradition. Holidays always gave me nervous butterflies. Underneath all the joy and excitement lies fear. Holidays mean alcohol is present.

The sun had set and we made it home. The Christmas lights from the tree sparkled reds, blues, and greens with tinsel. The smell of a sappy tree and cinnamon lingered in our cold house with the heater running, drying out our noses. My brother and I were checking out our Christmas gifts when we suddenly heard screaming.

We ran into the living room where I found my dad choking my mother. Her eyes were welted up with tears and her face was red as she struggled and begged him to stop.

"Look at what you did. Look what our kids have to see," he said as he acknowledged our presence. My brother and I cried, screaming for him to stop. At some point, my mother ran off and I heard the front screen door slam shut. My dad chased her outside, running alongside Highway 14, screaming that he would kill her when he caught her. It was dark outside and I couldn't see her anymore. I just collapsed on the hardwood floor hoping she got away.

We called my grandmother to come over. I remember my tiny grandmother tucking her 6'4" son into bed. My mom eventually called to tell me she was safe at a friend's house. I never remembered the next day from moments like that. I never understood how everything would go back to normal and life just continued on, whenever these moments occurred again.

Brick 27

I was around the age of nine when my mom left town for a few months for work. It must have been summertime because I don't remember being in school. Many nights my brother and I would be stuck at home or at a stranger's house with their kids. We would be left alone for hours, while my dad and a woman went out to drink. It was always a different woman. One night, I learned how to change a diaper since out of the five of us kids who had been left there, I was the one who volunteered. The youngest had a diaper so full and heavy that it eventually fell off of her. I figured it must be similar to when playing with baby dolls, so I put a new one on her. Later that night when our parents came home, I wasn't feeling well and went to find my dad. When I opened the door, I found him in bed with the other kids' mother.

We were home one afternoon and it was a beautiful, sunny day. My dad had just come out of the shower and had a towel around his waist. My brother tossed the cat outside, and the cat landed on his feet. The cat was not hurt in any way but this set my dad off. A switch was flipped and he aggressively started shutting the blinds and said, "I don't want the neighbors to see what I am about to do to you."

He started hitting my brother. The towel fell off and he didn't stop. I fell to the floor screaming and crying, covering my eyes. My dad ripped off my brother's necklace from my mom and flung it across the room. He was choking him and hitting him until his nose bled and then he threw him on the floor and walked away.

My brother scoffed at me, "What are you crying for? He didn't hit you."

Brick 31

After finally finishing my game of crying wolf, I put his belongings outside for the last time. The father of the twins was officially kicked out of my parent's house. He had lied to me for the last time and I finally broke things off. I was still so young, just 19 at the time. Most of my friends were still kids, while I was raising two of my own. Many people made comments to me, "I can't believe you kicked him out. How could you raise them without a dad?" I was determined for him to still be in their lives. No matter what excuse he threw at me, I had a solution.

If he didn't have a car seat or diapers, I would provide it so that he didn't have an excuse. "They are going to have a father in their lives," I would say as I handed him a packed diaper bag. He was less and less available and there wasn't anything else I could do to force him into being a dad.

A year later I received a message on Facebook. "I think it is terrible that you don't allow the twins to be in his life," said his newest girlfriend. After explaining that she had the story all wrong, that I never stopped him from being in their lives, suddenly dates were being set to meet at the park. It was a Wednesday afternoon and I was making sure their bag was packed well for a visit with their dad and his girlfriend. He called and said, "Hey, she was really trying to push the whole dad thing on me, sorry. I broke up with her, so we can just cancel the plans."

Brick 36

I was sitting nervously outside of a courtroom, alone, as the father of my daughter and his mother stared at me. I took a deep breath and anxiously fidgeted with my notes. I was going to represent myself. I was a single mom who could barely afford rent, let alone a lawyer. We were fighting over custody. It was an ugly situation and I had no one in my corner. His family would threaten to not give back my daughter, in the fear that I would move away and never contact them again. They were spiteful, not helpful. It was a war, not a village coexisting to raise a child. Stories were made up and painted my character to be less than. I was never offered help, as they only sought my demise.

Their lawyer confidently walked over and sat next to me as they watched. He leaned in and said, "They are paying me good money, because I am a good lawyer. I know you think this is going to be easy and fair but it's not. I have every intention of winning the best case scenario for my client, which means taking your daughter away from you and granting him 100% custody. I will win, and you will never see her again. Or, you can agree to 50/50 right now with no child support."

I signed.

Brick 39

I am meeting him for a drink after work. His cigarette hangs from his lips and he gleams as he looks over the photos he took on his new camera. This was something we shared, a passion for photography and late night whiskey. It had only been a few weeks but it felt so easy and fun. As I look at the long exposure shots, he kisses my neck and runs off to the bathroom. Our night would just be getting started. I admired how creative he was and how sweet it was to see the excitement light up his face. Suddenly, the night shots turned into photos of his kids. He seemed like such a great father. The next photo was his son kissing a pregnant belly. My mind skipped over the worst and I stupidly thought it was weird that his son would kiss someone's pregnant belly... unless, wait. No way.

My second thought was, maybe these are old photos from the past, but then I remembered that his camera was brand new. He walked out of the bathroom smiling. I was not smiling. "What is this?" I asked. He informed me that she was due any day. "I thought you knew," he muttered as he casually sipped his whiskey. I didn't know. He never told me but instead painted a picture of being a single dad that was recently divorced. I felt sick to my stomach and knew it had to be over. I was that other woman.

Brick 44

I found myself dating another guy who was in the middle of a divorce. I felt like I could relate because I had an ugly split too and it's very difficult starting over. People get hurt when their ex moves on, especially if kids are involved. I felt like I had met someone as lost as I was. He quickly became my best friend and things moved fast. I was always told that we had to keep things a secret because he and his ex-wife were still friends. She was codependent and scared to be alone and he didn't want to hurt her even more. I ignored the red flags because he even had me come over to meet his mother.

Things were getting serious until one night at work. She came to the bar I had been working at and as her friend shook her head at me saying, "Shame on you," I was punched in the back of the head. I towered over her as I was nearly a foot taller, being 5'10". My first instinct was to fight back but I could see how hurt she already was. "You should be punching him, not me," I said, as the security guards took her off the property.

After trying to end the relationship with him that night, he convinced me that she was just upset because he had moved on and she couldn't let go. But a few nights later a mutual friend called me, saying they saw them together. Suddenly I realized that I was the other woman, again. I was done. When he caught wind that I moved on, he sent me a video of the thoughtful gifts I had given him thrown into the river. I still see them together at the grocery store once in a while.

Brick 53

My heart was racing and my chest was tight, making it difficult to get a full breath of air. I was used to feeling arrhythmias and high heart rates but this time was different. I felt like I was fighting for my life. I begged for time to speed ahead and for help to come. Finally, when a doctor was present and I was more stable, I started to recite my cardiac history and asked to be put on the monitor so they could see what was going on. The doctor crossed his arms and leaned back. He smirked, then laughed.

"This is just anxiety," he said as he walked away. I wasn't put on a monitor or given an EKG, despite the scars on my chest. I was sent home. During this time, I went to the ER 52 times in one year. Little did that doctor know, I had a cardiac monitor under my sweatshirt. To catch what was going on, I had been wearing a monitor for weeks. After correlating the dates with this visit, and the other ER visits that followed the anxiety label in my patient history, I learned these episodes were more serious arrhythmias that would eventually land me with a pacemaker.

Brick 57

I finally found someone who loves me for who I am. There are no dark layers to peel. He loves my broken heart and accepts my complex dynamic of health issues and three children with two different fathers. Everything felt so easy.

We were having dinner at a holiday family gathering. His mother would often repeat the same conversation, as if to make sure we didn't miss it. "He would make such a great father," she said, as my children pushed around her bland food on their plates. "I am already a great father," he said. He loves my children as if they were his own. Even though we had discussions about having children, and she knew that I could not have any more, her comments still stung.

A year passed by and I was suddenly faced with a diagnosis of cervical cancer. I was so afraid. I had a friend reach out that also had cervical cancer and she wasn't doing well. She later passed away. I noticed a lot of women are afraid to talk about it. In online support rooms, the outcome looked grim. I knew if I needed chemo that my heart would not handle it. "Don't get a hysterectomy. The womb is a woman's second heart," his mom pleaded, in hopes there was still a chance I could provide her a grandchild that shared her blood.

Fortunately, the hysterectomy contained the cancer and I needed no further treatments, besides therapy to deal with a woman who would never think I'd be good enough for her son.

※ ※ ※

Looking back, as I reread my collection of writing that spans from my teen years through my early thirties, my perspective has changed a lot. I wish I could tell those versions of my younger self that everything would be okay. I used to think my dad was a monster. I told him once that he was. When I was 19, and again at age 32, I told him that he ruined my life. I put the consequences of my lack of coping onto him, blaming his behavior for how I handled life. What many of us fail to see is that life is both ugly and beautiful.

I was so lost in blaming my dad for my misery that I started to drown my feelings in alcohol. I also started to get angry and lose my cool. Instead of hating him, I decided to love him despite the mistakes he made. We all have our own circumstances and upbringing that evoke certain behaviors, until we learn to rewire our brain. Sometimes behavior is the product of a response. Hurt people hurt others because they don't know how to cope, or they don't have the proper tools to work through a problem.

I always like to imagine that I have an invisible mirror when someone treats me poorly. I imagine that the mirror is a wall between us and it is facing them. As they say hurtful things, they are instead looking at themselves in the mirror, not me. They are talking to themselves in a way. That harm isn't meant for me, but it's a way to outwardly drain their emotions. It's a release. I choose not to take anything personal and tell myself that they are hurting. As difficult as it may be, I use this thinking process to take others' emotions with a grain of salt.

When I think about each brick in my life that contributed to this wall I built, I now realize that each person who hurt me was also lost in life; they were coping with their own shit. I wasn't perfect myself. I know I contributed many bricks to other people's walls. I hurt others too. I was blinded by heartache and couldn't see that I could also be toxic. I didn't see it because I made justifications for my actions, as many of us do. I could look back at people who hurt me and hold a place of hate for them in my heart, but I don't want to carry that anymore. I forgive them because they were not healthy. Healthy people don't lie and hurt others. We all do things we regret, we hurt others, and we fuck up. Sometimes we even hurt ourselves.

I was in the crosshairs of their mistakes and painful journey of self discovery. There were people along my path who were also hurt by my actions when I was lost too. We have to remember to acknowledge that everyone has been a toxic person in someone's life, even if it was a misunderstanding. No one is exempt. We are all healing on different levels and some of us get stuck or lost along the way.

FIVE

Chronically Unwell

"'Cause she knows that
It'd be tragic
If those evil robots win"
-Yoshimi Battles the Pink Robots, Pt. 1 by The Flaming Lips

Mornings are hard. When you think of Sundays, you may think of sleeping in and waking up as the warm light finds its way to you. As you sit up, you give yourself a nice stretch and take a moment to admire the open window sharing hints of a beautiful day. If you live with chronic pain, the reality is that you wake up *because of* pain. You likely have woken up several times already, but you hurt too much to go back to sleep. For me, lying in bed hurts. It isn't this relaxing thing where I can leisurely sprawl out in bed and feel like I am on a cloud, melting into my mattress. No, I have to move because one position makes my tailbone go numb, another position hurts my collarbone, and lying on my stomach makes my back feel broken.

When I get out of bed everything pops back into place. Almost everything. My left hand and lips are tingling and numb

43

but it only lasts a few minutes. I walk to the bathroom, holding on to everything I pass for stability, so that I don't fall. My vision goes dark but I keep walking because I know I won't fully pass out. Even when I sit down, reaching to wipe is excruciating and demoralizing at times. It breaks me sometimes, glimpsing into the future and wondering if I will need help wiping my own ass one day. Then, as much as I want to crawl back into bed and snuggle up to my significant other, I quietly walk out of the room so I can find something to do and walk off the pain of sleeping.

My head is killing me and I am nauseous; it's as if I'm hungover from the tequila shots I never had. As I walk into the kitchen, everything fades away and I can't see. My body starts to feel fuzzy and go numb, just like before passing out. I can hear the whooshing of my blood moving from each heartbeat. I don't typically fully faint so I know that I can just keep walking through it as long as I hold on to the walls and furniture around me. I am a professional and have smiled and held conversations while on the brink of passing out, but I know it usually passes and this is my norm. This is all day, everyday.

When my pain levels are high, my morale is low. High pain days trigger my dysfunctional nervous system and make everything spiral out of control. My dreams and ambition slide over to the back burner. Sometimes they even get put away into Tupperware to decay in the back of the refrigerator, hidden behind the fruit. Sometimes the sunshine creeping in through the window looks so far away. *Just get through this*, I tell myself. I hold on to the idea of my next good day, whenever that may be. I find hope in new remedies and whatever ways I can try to have control over my health, albeit a distraction. On the pain scale of 1-10, I have never been under a five. My one is a five, it's my baseline.

When I first get into bed, everything catches up and hits me hard. The absence of sound is a piercing pitch that never ends. My muscles don't relax as they should but instead they have a mind of their own: spasms and twitching throughout and within my body, like fireworks. Every cell in my body aches. My breathing becomes shallow and short, as I remind myself to breathe every minute. My heart pounds so hard that it is followed by a rush to my head.

One of the many struggles with chronic illness is the unpredictability. It means starting each day off by spinning the *Wheel of Misfortune* and never knowing what symptom it will land on. It doesn't matter what was planned for the day when your body makes the rules.

Ignorance Truly is Bliss

I will never understand how people can't compute that you simply can't have a six figure career while in and out of hospitals your entire life. Chronic illness doesn't mean you are lazy. Someone who is chronically ill can still try to have a life, a career, a family, relationships, travel, hobbies, and a smile. It doesn't invalidate their illness. Just because you cannot see an illness doesn't mean it is not there.

If someone is sharing their story, it doesn't mean they seek attention. They want to be understood. They want to speak up for those who aren't able to share their story or those who are still discovering their voice. Many of those in the chronic illness community share their story because they understand what it feels like being lost and alone. We are all here for eachother.

If you hate someone or feel negatively about them, remove them from your life. If you don't understand someone and they anger you, why is this person in your life? Why do you watch, follow, or interact with them? Letdowns, uncertainties, anxiousness, feeling disheartened and isolated are many emotions that come with chronic illness. We suffer and still show up. We get knocked on our asses and still drag ourselves around until we can get back up. A chronic illness warrior's normal is your worst nightmare. I am fully convinced that if a healthy person were to live in the body of someone with chronic pain or chronic illness for just a day, they would fall to the floor in tears. I only say this as I have been attacked many times by people, even family, who didn't believe me, called me a hypochondriac, lazy, and even a mooch.

Chronic illness is a thief in so many ways. It will sneak in even when you least expect it, on a good day, and steal your plans. It will derail your life and cancel your dreams, throwing hurdles each time you get back on your feet. Relationships erode with each cancelling phone call. The stars that designed my future slowly fade. Chronic illness is a hurricane. She dances her way into town. No matter how prepared you may be, you are never sure what to expect, what you may lose, and the uncertainty of what could be destroyed. The aftermath of it all wears you down and deprives you of your energy. When you finally recover and rebuild, another storm comes.

But we do it over and over again, and will continue to do so. We aren't called warriors for nothing.

As the World Turns (Cardiac Ablation #2, circa 2003)

I'm not even old enough to buy a beer, yet and here I am lying on a cold metal table with my breasts exposed for all to see. My arms are strapped down and all I want to do is cover up my chest. I'm shivering from the cold room, and I can't feel my fingers. I'm nervous, staring at the metal tray that holds the instruments that will cut through my veins. All of the doctors are draped in a boring green. Maybe it was blue. Strangers in vinyl gloves and face masks. A radio is blaring. "We're going to sedate you just a little at first, because we need you to stay awake until we find the spot in your heart that we need to burn," the anesthesiologist explains.

I feel the drugs slithering throughout my body, my legs heavy and dead on the hard table. My back was uncomfortable but it isn't now. More drugs. My body, strapped down, slowly stops shaking from nervousness. I am wide awake but at least my muscles are sleeping. I am staring at a black and white screen. "We're going into your heart through a vein...you're going to feel this."

Suddenly I feel pressure and the screen I was staring at now has a picture that I cannot make out. It's the inside of my heart.

I lie there trapped inside my own body listening to doctors talk and music in the background. My heart slows down, I feel like I am going to die. I'm still cold. They speed it up... I feel like I am going to die. Hours go by. "Stop! Please! I can't stand this!" I cried. I haven't moved an inch and I am dizzy from the roller coaster they are putting my heart through.

"Why is she still talking?"

"I don't know. We gave her the max, she should be out by now."

"Well give her more."

"Alright....goodnight!" the doctor smirked at me as I slowly faded away from the noise, the coldness of the room, the screen of my heart, the smell of iodine and sterile equipment, and the feeling of my heart being controlled by someone else.

I woke up the next morning screaming. Two nurses, one on each side. Three maybe. One was holding a bed pan filled with vomit. I'm screaming again. My head feels like the worst hangover anyone could ever imagine. The vein in my leg, sore from hours of being open and stuffed with tubing to reach my heart. A simple procedure that takes an hour turned into six.

To stop the bleeding, the two nurses had to take turns pushing their weight to make enough pressure on my vein. I'm screaming at them, my head, my veins, the pain. I'm vomiting, I'm seeing stars. I'm naked in a nightgown on whatever floor, next to a bald old woman who is dying from cancer. Suddenly all I can think about is that I am interrupting her daytime television show.

The Grey Area

The grey area is a state which does not belong to one side or the other. It is nomadic and intermediate; the blurry line.

The grey area is where many undiagnosed, dismissed, and neglected health issues live. For some, they get tossed back and forth between doctors and never really helped by any, or are just getting by with the small crumbs of progress over a span of time.

The grey area is also the wait. It's waiting for the inevitable, irreversible, and impending progression of a particular diagnosis, searching for validity. It's knowing the risks but having no control or peace of mind.

The grey area is where the people who don't fit in the one-size-fits-all category call home.

Many of us only know the grey area, constantly hoping someone will understand us or send out a rescue team to bring us in. Some of us are yet to be diagnosed. Some aren't believed, while others can't even afford healthcare.

Awareness is for those looking to fit in somewhere, to make sense, to have answers, to not be neglected or alone. Share your fire until it lights up the sky, defining a new meaning and growing into a new path where those who were once lost can be found.

Open Heart Surgery

In early 2011, I was in the hospital for nearly a week. I was becoming depressed, as usual. Being in a hospital room always felt like what I'd imagine prison is like. You sit in this isolating room with an oversized uncomfortable gown, wires all over your chest with stickers that slowly eat away at your skin. There is constant beeping, no privacy, and every time you finally fall asleep they wake you up for blood work or vitals. My window view was the other side of the hospital, more windows of other patient's rooms with their blinds closed because they were too sick or tired to let the sun in.

"What is going on? I have been held here for a week and it's not like we are even waiting on more tests or anything," I asked for the third time.

Two heart surgeons came into my room. One was pacing and the other one was scratching his chin. We will call them Dr. A and Dr. B. They tell me I need open heart surgery.

Dr. B paces the room and says, "Look, you aren't a car. We can't just lift the hood and fix you. It's more complicated than that."

I ask, "Why not? My quality of life sucks. I am twenty-six and can barely chase around my kids without getting short of breath. This isn't how life should be."

Dr. B says, "You are young. There are risks and if you die on my table, your family will go after me and sue me. If an eighty year old dies on my table, well, they were just old."

Suddenly it sinks in that I have no one fighting for me and I don't stand a chance.

Dr. A finally speaks, "I will do it. I can replace that valve. You know, it's a nine inch incision on your chest, down your sternum. I mean, I don't really know what is causing this but, uh," his eyes are zoned out and he is searching for thoughts, "yeah, we can schedule this."

Clearly Dr. A and Dr. B are both not confident in this surgery. The only thing I can think of right now is to get out of there and start looking for a badass surgeon who knows what they are doing.

They discharged me from my week-long stay and instructed me to come to Dr. A's office to set up an appointment to begin preparing for open heart surgery. I go home and start researching and looking for better answers. I discovered heart-valve-surgery.com and created an account, just like you do for any other social media accounts.

I read other journals from people just like me. There were comments with hope, encouragement and advice. I made my first post and for once, I didn't feel alone. I learned more from that community of patients than from any pre-op appointment or doctor.

Then, I saw a recommendation from the "badass" doctor that I knew I needed. I was worried that surgery wouldn't be possible, due to finances and insurance. With my luck this guy was on the other side of the country. I was definitely dreaming for the best and was getting my hopes up because this was the only way. No one else was going to try and if they did try, they weren't confident. So, there he is: world renowned Dr. Kevin Accola. I click to find out more and guess what!? He is just an hour away! Other people were flying in from all over the country and for me, he was just the next county over.

The next thing I know, I am sitting in his chair and he says, "Wow, this is such an interesting case. I can't wait to get in there and see what is going on. What day do you want to schedule your surgery?" He smiles.

I nearly cried. After seven years, just like that, we booked the surgery. I never even got nervous, just pure excitement. When I was about to prepare for the surgery, he came in to say hi. He showed me my mechanical aortic valve but said that he would do everything he could to avoid it. He was aiming for a repair and would only do a three inch incision instead of the standard nine.

He was able to do the repair and avoid the mechanical valve which came with a life of blood thinners and replacements. He was a badass.

Pacemaker

The frigid air makes my hands turn white
and numb as my body shivers.
My back is against the icy hard table,
hands strapped down.
Bright lights.
Beep... beep... beep. Drip...drip... drip.
I feel the cold saline run through my veins
while I try to focus my vision.
Breathe. Just breathe.
My body shakes. Focus.
Everything is going to be okay. Asleep.
Awake.
The steel blade glides down my pale skin
as dark ruby red spills over.
I look into my doctor's eyes and say, "Hey, I'm awake."
"No you're not," she says. I argue back, "But I am,"
and watch her blade pull away.
I tell her that I feel everything,
"Don't worry, it doesn't hurt," I say.
"No you can't... Get her back to sleep!"
"Why is she so alert?" the nurse asks. More drugs.
I ask how everything is going
as they push more medicine into my veins.
The nurse stares into my eyes, hoping I close mine.
The room gets fuzzy, but only for a second.
I can breathe and the shivering stops.
I nervously talk. Deep breath.
Everything ends abruptly, like the end of a movie.
Then, the curtains rise and suddenly
I'm in another bright room.
The pain throbs and my heart races,
like a hummingbird.
Seeing stars, feeling the agony,
dreading the coming hours.
I just want to go back to sleep.

Keep Going

I am having a relaxing day; the warm sun comes through my window and I feel happy, until suddenly my head feels like I got hit by a metal baseball bat. I jump up out of bed in a panic while trying to assess what is happening to me. My right ear and head are buzzing intensely like an electric shock. My trembling palms become clammy. My heart rate shoots up, more than doubling what it was and I become disoriented. My head feels like it is going to implode with pins and needles. I dial 911, take slow deep breaths to stay calm, then fumble around for the aspirin. *Breathe.* I try to remember my birthday and how to speak when the operator asks questions. "Just come."

It's days like this that make me feel like a prisoner in my own body. To be a medical anomaly is isolating, making you feel desperate and hopeless. I was just daydreaming about being in nature and how happy I was to feel better than I did yesterday. I would be lying if I didn't say that these moments often make me question whether I will make it through the day. *Will I have a stroke or go into cardiac arrest? Will I see my husband and children again? What will they do when I am gone?*

No, I can't. I won't!

My thoughts swirl in a panic, as I fight through the episodes. When everything is calm and over, I spend the next few days in fear. I worry about having another vestibular or dysautonomia episode. My bed, which is my safe place, suddenly doesn't feel so safe. I find myself worried about watching the same thing on TV that I was watching when the episode hit, or I become afraid to eat whatever I ate that day. I had one of my favorite meals at my favorite local restaurant. *What if it was triggered by my meal?* Irrational thoughts take over my mind until days pass and I slowly lighten up.

To make matters worse, most doctors are not well versed in rare illnesses and it is likely outside of their scope of work. It can be very isolating to feel dismissed, neglected, and deemed a hypochondriac by medical professionals and loved ones. For me, I hit a fork in the road and had to choose: keep going and advocate for myself, or give up. I chose to keep going. My heart aches for those who don't.

There were times I felt helpless, especially when I didn't have health insurance. I felt like I had no one on my side. Medical professionals dismissed me, as this was a time before social media and awareness on rare diseases existed. I had no one to relate to. We are lucky to live in a time where we can connect with others from across the globe. Now, we can click a hashtag of our disorders and fall down a rabbit hole of people who share the same rare diseases. We all have people who can relate if we just look hard enough. I lived in an era where I was alone, being a young girl with heart issues. With the Internet today, I am never alone. I hold so much gratitude and love for my online friends, many of whom I may never meet in person.

SIX

Do No Harm

*"I tried to scream
But my head was underwater
They called me weak
Like I'm not just somebody's daughter"*
-everything e wanted by Billie Eilish

Marijuana Cigarette

I remember the nurse ripping the curtain open and walking towards me. She grabs my gown and puts her hands down the gown and onto my bare chest, tearing the cardiac leads off of me.

"What's going on?" I asked.

"Well, we can't help you because you had a marijuana cigarette in your blood system."

This was just as the laws were passing in Florida and legal marijuana was still very new. The stigma was still heavily enforced. In the eyes of this nurse I was just a drug addict smoking the devils cabbage. They were not going to take me seriously and they were not going to look any further, despite 20 years of health records in that ER with never a single positive drug test (besides cannabis).

Many doctors assumed that with my tattoos and how I looked, it was more likely that my valves were damaged from drug use rather than a genetic disorder. Medical bias was always against me. Being born with heart issues, the idea of drugs scared me and I had no interest. Somehow, my chronic fatigue, brain fog, disorientation from vestibular issues, weight fluctuations, statistics and attention seeking pain made me look like a drug addict. I have always been someone who would take a hot tea and a bath rather than a pain pill. After surgeries, I rarely take pain meds or opioids that are prescribed because they make my chronic constipation worse, give me vivid nightmares, and they cause my depression to get worse.

Many people with chronic pain and Ehlers-Danlos syndrome take opioids because their pain is so unbearable. It's not always easy to make these decisions, but for some, their quality of life depends on it. For me, cannabis helps to keep me calm so that I don't drown from suffering. Each patient is different, yet I will never understand why we are all treated the same.

Even if I were a drug addict, as everything in my life could have led me down that path, I should not have been treated that way. My care should not have ever been dismissed. No one should be sent away, even if their pain is emotional. Everyone needs help sometimes. If you are going to have a career in healthcare then you MUST have compassion. Help others and do no harm.

23

Trigger Warning: Suicide, Blood, Abuse

I felt so remorseful. The adrenaline has worn off as did the shock of reality. I couldn't believe I had done this to myself, but I still felt angry over the hopelessness of the situation. I still didn't see a way out yet and I knew that what I had just done was not going to make it better. I had a white towel wrapped around my arm; being someone who is in and out of the ER so often I knew where to look when no one would bring me one. The color of my blood against the clean white towel was so vibrant. Every few minutes somebody would come in but only to take a look at me and leave. I sat there for a long time, with my wounds wide open. Someone else came into the room, took a peek and left again. I felt like a sideshow freak. After hours of waiting, a nurse finally came in to start cleaning the wounds. It stung and burned and so I made a face and a sound as I was reacting to the pain.

"Can you please be gentle?" I apprehensively asked the nurse. "It hurts."

"Why?" she asked. "You did this to yourself."

The doctor came in and was not amused. I was just a stupid girl wasting his time when there were real emergencies. He was humming a song as he stapled my arm back together. He stapled so sloppily that I had a staple in my skin for no reason. There was not even a wound around it. It was just a lost staple that was blatantly shot into my arm. There were 23 other staples. The doctor never made eye contact with me but after he finished humming his song he turned away and left the room. Another nurse had a little more compassion as she saw the tears roll down my face. She had to remove a few staples and redo a few areas that were so poorly done. I had to go up to the second floor of the hospital, which was a psychiatric floor, where I'd spend the next 72 hours of my life. I was so angry and I refused to speak. I knew nobody would understand me. I spent the first day not speaking and not eating. In one room, a girl cried and wailed as she ripped out her hair, throwing it onto the floor next to a crumpled up magazine that contained photos of smiling women.

In the main room an older woman walked around stealing the phone from whoever was using it and taking people's food off of their plates. There was also a guy that looked to be about my age, maybe a year or two younger, who came over and sat down next to me. He had dreadlocks and asked me why I was there. He told me, "You better eat your food and you better start talking, or you won't get out of here. I understand that you don't wanna be here but I have been here before, and I know the tricks to this place." My ears perked up and I was ready to pick up the shitty cafeteria hospital food and shovel it into my mouth. I wanted to get home to my children and I wanted to get the fuck out of that place. The rooms had no windows and we all had roommates. There was only one window at the end of the hall.

I was able to leave after 72 hours. I did everything I was supposed to and even said I was feeling better, though it was just a ploy to go home. I threw away the knife set but I kept the one knife. I kept that knife for years...until one day the handle finally broke off. I would use it to slice tomatoes, to open packages, to cut up my dinner...It was a reminder of how dangerous it can be to live in the dark. I never wanted to get that low again.

The part that hurts the most looking back, is that those 72 hours didn't do anything for me mentally. I needed help so desperately and I would continue to need help for far too many years to follow. There was never talk about postpartum depression,

I had no counseling, and I had no money to even afford therapy. It was just a waiting game to go back. Still, somehow it wasn't a wake up call. Instead my focus was on coming home to pack up everything I own and move into an apartment, away from the emotionally abusive person who regularly told me I was worthless. That month, I juggled three jobs so that I could save enough money for the first and last months' rent and deposit on a new place to live.

When I look back, I realize I can't believe I pulled that off or that I was able to make that happen. At the time I felt like I was still such a failure to even have to be getting out of such a situation. Even as I share my story, I cringe at what people might think, those who don't know this side of me. What I realize is that as much as I believed I didn't care about what others think, I guess somehow I do. Maybe we all do a little, as we were praised or punished based on our behavior as children. I still struggle to retrain my brain about the stigma of mental health and how others still continue to judge. As a whole, collectively, not everyone is there yet. We are still a divided nation struggling to educate others on mental illness, and help them to find the compassion to understand diversity.

During that time in my life, I was suffering from postpartum depression, PTSD, and reading Sylvia Plath didn't help. I was in an unstable environment, living with someone who threatened to have his way with me. He told me how horrible of a mother I was on a regular basis. I already felt worthless but anytime I felt a glimmer of light, I was reminded that I belonged in the dark. At that point in my life, I felt isolated and alone. I had no one, or at least I thought that. I called women's shelters and they were full. He was standing there, in his underwear.

Tears rolled down his face as he spewed hurtful words. In an attempt to feel strong and in control, I said something hurtful back, calling him a child and telling him to wipe the snot off of his face. He backhanded me. I ran for my phone to call someone and arrange a place to stay. That person was drinking and at a bar so I hung up. I threw my silenced phone under my bed. I went straight to the kitchen.

I looked down at my arm, my veins staring at me. I grabbed a knife and went numb. I told myself, "you are doing them a favor." I looked up at him and lost myself in his eyes. I hoped he would see how much his years of effort would pay off. Five times, I ran the knife over my arm, hoping I would hit the right spot as I wasn't looking. I broke eye contact as I entered back into the present moment. The knife dropped onto the floor as my blood spilled onto the white tiles.

"*Nooooooooooo.....*" *What did I do?* My skin opened up and I could not believe what I had done.

Odyssey

In a lengthy letter to another doctor, the point was made to mention my young children, "crying and slamming toys around during the entire appointment." This report was back in 2005 when my twins were in their terrible twos phase. She paints a clear picture of a young mother that is exhausted and stressed. Though I have had symptoms since my childhood, well before being a tired mother, it is portrayed as if my symptoms were caused by the stress of being a new mother. This is a letter that my other doctors will refer to in my charts. It's their first impression of me through the eyes of a doctor who has a patient outside of her scope, yet is too confident in her experience and education to ever admit that. I once had an ER doctor joke that I was there to get a break from my kids. That couldn't be further from the truth, and it only made me feel more worthless.

There are mentions of cardiac issues that were very apparent and noted that they were "dismissed due to the patient not complaining" when really, I didn't know how to describe what I was complaining about. Maybe I didn't complain because this was all I knew. It was my normal. An example of this is the diagnosis at the age of 16, of "Pott's Disease," which is mentioned by many doctors in different notes and spelled this same way. Pott's Disease is a form of tuberculosis that occurs outside of the lungs. What the doctor meant was POTS, which is short for Postural Orthostatic Tachycardia Syndrome. Not only is this a great example of diagnostic error that spread to a handful of doctors, but it is an example of what they later dismissed because I complained more about tachycardia (which is the T in POTS) so they focused on that and threw out the diagnosis. Why? Because it was simpler. Another example of being dismissed is when my doctor noted that my heart rate was in the 30s and chose to dismiss it since "the patient didn't mention the episode." However, the time stamp shows that I was clearly sleeping at 3:00 a.m. How would I have known that my heart dipped so low while asleep?

These little crumbs are sprinkled throughout my health history, passed over and swept away over time. What these doctors didn't understand about my complex undiagnosed illness was simply brushed aside. No one stepped up to dig deeper, to do genetic testing, or to find out what cause the heart of a twenty year old to become enlarged on one side, have a severely insufficient aortic valve, tachycardia, bradycardia, arrhythmias, chest tightness, shortness of breath, fatigue, fibromyalgia, sleep apnea, IBS, chronic pain, and at that time, two cardiac ablations for supraventricular tachycardia.

It took seven years to finally get my aortic valve repaired. Before the repair, I had two more ablations, totaling four cardiac ablations, to get rid of the fast heart rates. I had multiple ER visits, doctors appointments, hospitalizations, and doctor after doctor kept pushing me away, telling me it was all just stress.

There was another time when I had a carotid artery ultrasound done. Being impatient and not wanting to wait three weeks until my follow-up appointment, I went to the facility where I had the test done and requested the report. The report noted that I had multiple tumors on my thyroid and to "please advise the patient to follow up with an endocrinologist." When my appointment came and I met with my cardiologist, he held the report in his hands, the same report I had read, and he looked at me and said, "It's great. All normal." That was the day I learned to start reading every report, to keep all my records and to begin advocating for myself. I remember leaving the office feeling so betrayed. It felt as if I found a phone number in my boyfriend's pocket. *How could he lie to me? Why?* The next day, I picked myself up and made an appointment to see an endocrinologist.

Another time, I was in the ER complaining of stomach issues. They did a CT scan of my abdomen and eventually said everything was fine and discharged me. Well, you know me by now, and you better believe I had those records in my hand the next day. This was the day I discovered my right fallopian tubal clip had dislodged and relocated to the right side of my body, into my abdominal wall. This meant that I had a metal clip floating around my body, lodging itself into my organs. This also meant that every other month I could get pregnant. With the state of my health at the time, that would not be advised. No one ever mentioned this to me. Not my general physician, not the ER doctor, absolutely no one. I booked an appointment with my gynecologist the next week to get the clip removed.

There are dozens of examples I could list just from my own personal experience. The statistic is that one in twenty people are misdiagnosed, according to a 2014 study published in the journal BMJ Quality and Safety. That averages out to nearly twelve million people per year. If you are a patient, always get another opinion if you don't feel confident in the diagnosis. Research the diagnosis so that you are educated and fully understand. This may help you to realize that a diagnosis really does fit or you may realize it might be wrong. I can't count how many times I have had conversations with others about their health and they don't even know the name of their diagnosis. I can't wrap my head around that! Write it down. Keep a journal or folder with symptoms, dates for tests, research, records and anything else you need to remember. This is your health! If you can remember your favorite team or the name of your favorite paint color, then you should know the names of your medication and diagnosis, and know them well. You are a 15 minute appointment to some doctors. But, you go home and then it's all you. It's the rest of your life and you know your body more than anyone else.

If you are a physician and you have a patient that has unusual symptoms, nothing seems to connect or add up, and there is no obvious answer, send them to someone else that would be a better fit. Do not, I repeat: DO NOT waste their precious time dismissing them and not helping them, or perhaps not believing them. With places like Mayo Clinic and Cleveland Clinic, or learning hospitals in your area, there is absolutely no excuse to hold their health hostage in your hands because your ego can't admit that they are outside of your scope.

I'm Not Convinced

"I'm not convinced."

Those were the words out of my decade-long relationship with my trusted electrophysiologist, whom I will refer to as Dr. J. I saw her on and off for 10 years during the moments I had health insurance. I had 4 cardiac ablations for supraventricular tachycardia (SVT) from a rare congenital heart disorder called Wolff-Parkinson-White Syndrome, which is an extra electrical conduction pathway between chambers that causes arrhythmias. My heart rates would go up into the 300's and drop down into the thirties. After four cardiac ablations and still having arrhythmias and fast heart rates, I could not take meds to slow down my heart since my rate would drop low too. I spent years in that position, in limbo, without treatment and living with a chaotic heart.

My valves began to deteriorate as well, causing even more issues. I had open heart surgery for an aortic valve repair and will need a valve replacement in the future, requiring open heart surgery again. My trusted electrophysiologist told me that it sounded like I was dealing with something that was too rare and not likely possible. She wasn't convinced I could have another rare disorder. She denied me treatment. I was afraid to sleep at night, afraid that I wouldn't wake up. Did you know you can pass out in your sleep? I had finally collected my most recent fifty page heart event monitor report from the vice president of the device company, since my doctor would not give me the reports. I posted my heart rhythms on Facebook, begging for anyone who knows anything to help me. Many people reached out, nurses and firefighters, saying those episodes were not normal. Finally, a friend tagged another friend, who sent me a private message. She worked for an electrophysiologist in the area and could make me an appointment. After previously trying to leave my electrophysiologist, another one turned me away in fear of disrespecting Dr. J. I was so relieved to have a shot with the only other electrophysiologist in the area.

I took my records to a new physician, who then ordered a Tilt Table Test and induced an episode. He found that I had a severe cardioinhibitory response and confirmed that I needed a pacemaker. He said a pacemaker would also give me a safety net to keep my heart from falling under 60 beats per minute, treating the bradycardia and heart block. This also meant I could finally take heart medications to prevent my tachycardia and arrhythmia episodes without making my heart too slow. My new physician questioned why this hadn't been done yet, while notifying me that he was relocating in the next couple of weeks and would not be able to do the surgery. How the hell would I convince my previous doctor after seeking a second opinion?

A week later, I ended up in the ER and was admitted to the hospital. My heart was all over the place as usual. Dr. J was the on-call doctor and she was ready to send me home, despite my tilt table test results. She claimed that the test was outdated, barbaric, and not used in modern medicine anymore. She also stated that she was still "not convinced." From the dark hospital room, I called the second opinion electrophysiologist that told me I needed a pacemaker. My doctor was on her way to submit discharge orders. I explained to him that Dr. J would not give me a pacemaker and he told me this was his last day in the office before relocating seven hours away. He came over to the out-of-network hospital at his own leisure just to speak to her.

Even though she was not fully convinced, she agreed to implant a pacemaker due to such effort. The next week, my life changed. My heart rate doesn't pause, stop or plummet and I can take meds to keep my heart rate from going too high. The pacemaker even kicks in to reduce arrhythmias and blood pressure drops. I take medications now to reduce going into arrhythmias.

I will never forget the next day in the hospital after getting the pacemaker implant when the technician called her to give my first 24-hour report. The technician stated that the pacemaker was pacing at 97% and a few times it kicked in to prevent episodes, the very episodes of neurocardiogenic syncope that she didn't believe I had. She asked the technician, "Are you sure?"

"Yes, I am looking at the pacemaker interrogation now. I am sure," the tech said puzzled, wondering why she was questioning him.

I felt so validated.

The puzzle pieces all came together after seeing specialists and understanding why I was having a dysfunctional nervous system, irregular heartbeats, chronic pain, chronic fatigue, IBS, and an array of health issues. Genetic testing, research, and being my own advocate helped more than anything. It took my entire life to get answers. I finally learned that I have Ehlers-Danlos Syndrome, a connective tissue disorder that causes many of my health issues, on top of Wolff-Parkinson-White (WPW) Syndrome. Having WPW made it harder to see that something more could be going on because everyone was focused on that particular diagnosis. I still wonder, in awe, how it took 34 years to finally have a diagnosis. My medical records always stated, "the patient has a long list of unusual symptoms," and left it at that. No one looked deeper. I grew up trusting doctors and their oath to do no harm, but negligence is harm.

I never want anyone else to ever have to go through what I have gone through. I never want anyone else to be medically neglected, dismissed, or too rare for their doctor to be convinced. There is an entire world of people suffering in the dark. My mission is to change that. I raise awareness for those people that feel alone, lost and ignored while they fear for their lives, praying to wake up the next morning. I turned my frustrations into purpose, letting my fire pave the way for others.

I Am Not a Stoner

There are still people who think cannabis is a drug. Cannabis is a plant. There are still people who think cannabis users are "stoners." There are so many stigmas STILL tied to marijuana and there probably always will be.

I do not want to take opioids for chronic pain every day. I do not want to take anti-nausea medications daily for when I get low blood pressure drops, migraines, or from pain. I do not want to take the 3 medications given to me for gastrointestinal issues. I do not want to take muscle relaxers every day for my muscle spasms. I do not want to take benzos every day for my dysfunctional autonomic nervous system, muscle twitches, and to calm the never-ending tinnitus (ringing in my ear). I do not want to take daily meds for vertigo that stems from my vestibular issues.

One recent morning, my clammy hands shook as I hyperventilated because of the debilitating pain I was experiencing. I tried to catch my breath and focus on my hands to stop shaking so that I could take my medicine, cannabis, which replaces so many others I would need to take. Slowly, everything stops spinning and I can breathe. My jaw unclenches a little and my back relaxes after being so tense. I can wipe away my tears and put on a little makeup and go on with my day. I can breathe.

Besides one side effect of having food cravings, cannabis is not addictive and there are no potentially fatal withdrawal symptoms I would have to endure, unlike with some other medications. I occasionally do take those other medications when my health gets out of control or to an emergent level, but I am thankful for cannabis allowing me that choice.

I am not a stoner.

I AM...

- A hardworking mother and wife
- An entrepreneur
- A small business owner of my own self-care botanical product line called Wildling Apothecary
- A health advocate
- A biomedical science (BAS) student with a 4.0 GPA
- The founder of Blu Dream Health Collective, a nonprofit organization that utilizes social media, podcasts, and publishing to bring awareness to chronic illness and mental health.
- I am also a writer, a lover of art, a travel and adventure addict, a chronic illness warrior,

an open-heart surgery survivor, an alcohol-free badass and a legal marijuana patient.

PTMT - Post Traumatic Medical Trauma

Post Traumatic Medical Trauma is a post-traumatic response to medical related trauma, physiological or psychological stress due to a medical event, chronic pain, serious illness or injury. The fear of death, complexity of illness, grief, medical neglect, and other negative experiences can trigger a PTSD-like response.

A feeling takes over you, nuzzling into the pit of your stomach that buzzes out to your limbs. It's like you are standing at the edge of a cliff but there is no beautiful view, just a worry so strong that it consumes you. Your blood feels thick as it boils through your veins, dragging its gloom to the surface of your skin, begging to get out. This is the feeling that takes over your brain, your gut, and your heart. It's the aftershock of a traumatic event that creeps up on you, tapping you on the shoulder and pouring itself into your bones.

Post-Traumatic Medical Trauma is a name I thought of to put a title on a common feeling that many people with health issues can relate to. Health anxiety and depression from chronic illness are frequent concerns for many people.

Common Struggles for People
with Chronic Illness:

- Missing or grieving your previous, healthier life and adjusting to a change due to health issues
- Having to cancel on friends and family often or change plans because of health
- Feeling secluded and like no one understands you
- Financial issues due to lack of work or missing work from illness
- Feeling exhausted and having a hard time keeping up with minor tasks
- Not talking about how you feel or your feelings for the sake of not making others feel uncomfortable
- Being dismissed by medical providers or loved ones
- Traumatic medical experiences
- Brain fog
- Chronic pain and/or health issues
- Coping with an incurable disease or disorder
- Unsolicited medical advice
- Insurance issues, scheduling conflicts, and other general concerns

I often wonder why some doctors don't ask their patients how they are coping with their health issues. For some, they hide their anxiety or depression out of fear that their health issues will be dismissed and labeled as anxiety or stress. I have personally brushed over living with depression out of fear my issues would be blamed on stress. The golden standard should be that therapy or counseling is offered or suggested after a life-changing surgery or health event. Stress will absolutely make health issues worse or create a domino effect of new health ailments. I will always emphasize that you must give your body a fighting chance. While stress can sometimes be the answer, it is also an overused catch-all to idiopathic symptoms without a clear answer. This results in many patients, like myself, spending much of their lives living undiagnosed.

For me personally, my traumatic health memories sometimes follow me to bed and enter my dreams. Having a small health scare, like a few palpitations in a row, can trigger PTMT and put a damper on the rest of my day. Like a dark cloud following me around all day, I can't help but think of moments when my heart almost gave up for good. My lips turned dusky as everything around me faded out. My heart was struggling and chaotic as if each beat could be the last. My limbs were cold on the ground as I struggled to take tiny drops of air into my lungs. My life did not flash before my eyes, but a sinking feeling of worry about my kids growing up without a mother and, *how could I just meet the love of my life just to be taken from this world and my family that I love so much?*

It's not fair.

I am not ready yet.

Please.

Help.

Every palpitation I get is a flashback of these moments. Some days are so beautiful and the sun shines, blanketing everything in gold. The air is perfect and I have everything to be grateful for; but still, sometimes those moments tickle my neck because I am so scared to lose everything.

You are not alone.

Finding local or online support groups are helpful for finding answers and a community of others who understand what you have gone through, or what you may be going through. Seeking therapy is also a beneficial way to learn how to cope and work through stress. You are not alone. Burying your feelings or sweeping them under the rug is not a way to get by. Dealing with your trauma is nothing to be ashamed of or ignore. Mental health needs to be addressed prior to becoming critical or too late.

SEVEN

Narcissist

"I got just one life
In a world that keeps on pushin' me around
But I'll stand my ground
And I won't back down"
-I Won't Back Down by Tom Petty

A narcissist is an extremely selfish person who has an exaggerated sense of self-importance, a lack of empathy for others, and an uncanny way of manipulating people into serving their self-absorbed needs. Narcissists feel entitled and superior; they always need constant admiration, validation, gratitude, praise, and control over others. They have a very difficult time accepting feedback and criticism, are easily wounded, and quick to feel hurt or angry. They have a lack of interest in your qualities because their own interests are more important and valuable in their eyes. They will never accept fault or take the blame for anything, and if they do, the narcissist is somehow the victim and you end up apologizing instead of them. Those with Narcissistic Personality Disorder typically fantasize about their ultimate success and power, expect constant admiration, feel entitled to everything, exploit others, lack empathy, and have a larger than life sense of self-importance over others.

You will deeply regret bringing up an issue and ultimately give up, as the narcissist will never take ownership or responsibility for their mistakes. They also capitalize on exploiting sympathy; if you had a bad day, be prepared to hear how their day was worse. They will always dominate a conversation until you are blue in the face. You might walk away without ever even having the opportunity to say what you planned to discuss in the first place. This is due to the narcissist making the conversation go in circles until you are disoriented and mentally dizzy. Having a conversation with a narcissist usually results in sweeping everything under the rug after a failed attempt to resolve an issue. Many people who are victims of NPD have Complex PTSD and tend to shut down during confrontations with a narcissist. Those who have been raised by a narcissist, or spent time with one, may feel crippled from the narcissist's manipulative and controlling behavior due to a PTSD response.

Being "loved" by a narcissist is very stressful and frustrating, as the love they have is very conditional. You will be showered with love when you are pleasing them and making them happy; however, should you disappoint them, you will experience devaluation, verbal abuse, or a very cold shoulder. This behavior often manipulates you into giving the narcissist what they want so that you can be "loved" again or on good terms. This ultimately feeds and fuels their ego, sense of control and entitlement even more. If you open up to a narcissist, be prepared for any bits of information you fed them to be used to their advantage to exploit you. They will take your pain and insecurities to control the situation in their favor. They will bring up things from the past or remind you of favors they did for you in order to put you in your place. Remember, they always want to be praised so if they gave you a gift or did even the smallest favor, they will always hang it over your head. The gift is never for you but it is for their own selfish benefit: a debt you owe.

Gaslighting is a very common and expected form of manipulation that a narcissist carries in their toolbox. Gaslighting is a psychological manipulation by the narcissist to control you by making you question your own sanity, memory, and perception, leading you to doubt yourself. The confusion and mental fatigue leads you to give in or give up. The exhausting and stressful circles inevitably end with the narcissist creating doubt in the individual, making them question their own judgment by using tactics that feed on low self-esteem. Oftentimes, the narcissist will use something special to you as ammunition or control. They will wear you down and demolish the foundation of your existence, sucking you into believing that you forever owe them. Belittling and bullying you is a way to make themselves feel more important while your insignificance has you believing that they actually are. They will remind you that they aren't perfect and criticize you for focusing on their flaws rather than worshiping their existence. Or, they will point out all of your flaws to even the playing field. They never have any repercussions for their actions (nor are they ever held accountable), which enables their behavior even more. You will more often than not feel invalidated.

Should you be wronged by the narcissist, you will never get an apology. If you let them know that they hurt you in any way, take a seat and get your popcorn ready; you are in for a long ride. You are going to hear all about your past mistakes, your flaws, and be reminded of all that they have done for you. Once you start to feel worthless, you actually end up apologizing to them. You feel as though you have to repay them for whatever they dangle over your head. They have justified their behavior to the point where you don't even know what day it is. Now, they are hurt and you are the asshole. You apologize, they smile (as they got their way) and you hug. They walk away feeling superior and in control while you melt into your chair questioning yourself and your worth. The more this goes on, the less you complain or even dare to express your feelings.

You may find yourself walking on eggshells to avoid upsetting the narcissist. You will often bite your tongue after they insult you, knowing it is a battle you will never win. The emotional poison erodes the core of your being, leaving you as an empty shell. It's as if you become their puppet, their praising audience, or their doormat where they put all their weight on you to unleash their dirt before leaving you with the mess. Over time, you become broken down and well trained. Your relationship becomes an orchestrated symphony as the narcissist remains on their pedestal. There are times when you will be successful or shine, and the narcissist in your life will find a way to take credit somehow. They will pin the reason you are doing well on them. If someone else points out a positive or unique quality in you, the narcissist will also take credit, as anything good from you surely has come from them. The compliment must somehow be redirected to the narcissist, the original creator of all that is great.

Covert Narcissist

There are multiple subtypes of narcissistic personality disorder. Covert narcissists are basically the closeted introvert type that goes under the radar. Their shy, humble, and anxious personality tricks you into not realizing that you are getting worked over. At the end of the day, their behavior is a coping mechanism for insecurity and not feeling in control.

Six Signs that You May be Dealing with a Covert Narcissist:

1. They're overly sensitive to criticism. If you think you can let them know about an issue, think again. Watch out for blame-shifting and manipulative tactics. It's not quite like gaslighting, but an entirely different monster. Suddenly you will be questioning your character and doubting yourself over the picture they just tried to paint. They will decide to read your mind and are convinced that is their truth. You may not even know what is going on when they decide to shut down.

2. They put themselves down so that you can stroke their ego. They rely on others to build themselves up. Remember, they are shy and humble. It is your job to make them feel good about themselves. If you forget, their insecurities will trigger a reaction.

3. After the eighth time of tiptoeing around a question, you still haven't gotten a response. When you kindly ask one more time, you will be sorry. This person must feel in control and they must dictate the timeline. You're not allowed to ask questions…just sit in the corner in time out. They are the boss. They may suddenly decide to

work things out but only if they find a way to where they benefit.

4. They want to gain recognition without putting in the work. They feel tasks are beneath them. They fantasize about being an important influence and exaggerate their abilities.

5. They are passive aggressive. You will never know when there is an issue until it's too late. Part of the introvert's insecurity is to become withdrawn as a coping mechanism when they feel they aren't in control. When you try to communicate and find a solution, it may be impossible to resolve unless you just give in. This guessing game will drive you crazy. Try to stay cool, calm, and collected.

6. You will never know if you're doing something wrong because they'll smugly smile and nod. Later, you'll learn about all of your imperfections and mistakes, unbeknownst to you, when it's time for them to present their case of how they are victimized. Their customer service personality will smile and shine, but on the inside they are rolling their eyes at you. Instead of communicating about the little sparks, they let it build into a raging fire that inevitably burns everything down.

If you find you have a business partner, professional relationship, a friendship, a family member, an acquaintance, a significant other, or any other relationship type and you're stuck in the toxic pattern, find some help to work through it. Talking to a therapist is helpful to acknowledge the situation you are in, and how you can navigate this unhealthy relationship. For some, you may find you can't walk away.

Setting boundaries may be a helpful tool to avoid the trauma they inflict.

Though somehow this person may have convinced you that you're the bad guy, you'll find that they never really had any respect for you, nor any genuineness that exists in their soul. Protect yourself, as mental health can oftentimes spill over into your physical health. You cannot control how others behave or treat you but you can draw a line in the sand.

Getting Out of Their Cage

Narcissistic Personality Disorder causes are not well understood. Some researchers believe NPD stems from needing protection from their insecurities, a primal defense mechanism that began as a result of a trauma or situation in the past that left the individual with a deep emotional wound. Genetic, biological, and environmental factors may contribute to the disorder. Unfortunately, treatment is a tough challenge because a typical narcissist will be greatly defensive to accepting the diagnosis or treatment. A true professional and licensed therapist is always a good start to working through NPD, not just for the narcissist but also for the loved ones involved. The relationship can be exhausting, stressful, time consuming, and create anxiety or diminish self-worth in those affected. You may even become desensitized over the years to the reality of the situation. If the narcissist refuses to seek professional help, it's best that you still seek help for yourself in order to cope with the toxic relationship.

You may feel like you have met a fork in the road (in order to continue the relationship) when you are trying to find the balance of boundaries vs. the never-ending forced forgiveness flow of disregarded situations. You may not always have the opportunity to cut someone out of your life, so setting distinct and firm boundaries is crucial. Creating space is also helpful, though the narcissist will not usually allow or respect the request for space. In fact, they may pop up even more than usual; therefore, asking for space may be less of a success. Instead, create the space by answering less phone calls, becoming less available, engaging less, and creating a professional-like tone for the relationship. Stop adding fuel to the fire by engaging because you will never get your point across. Walk away.

By setting boundaries, you are teaching others how you expect to be treated. If they do not respect your boundaries then they may no longer have the opportunity to treat you poorly. We cannot control others but we can teach them where you draw the line. You should never give anyone the power to make you feel terrible about yourself. No one deserves the opportunity to control you.

A narcissist fails to acknowledge that they do not get to decide whether or not they hurt you. You get to decide when to say no, where to set boundaries, when to cut someone off, how you are going to let them affect you, and whether or not they have power over you. The trauma that happens in your life is a seedling; it can grow into something that takes over everything or it can grow into something simple and beautiful. It's not about the shitty people in your life that made you feel worthless, it's about overcoming that fragile state and taking your power back. No one should ever be allowed to make you feel a certain way.

NARCISSIST

I used to let people in my life decide for me how to feel, especially about myself. You have to find the courage to take charge of your life. Being prepared is a great tool for dealing with a narcissist. When time inches closer to making contact with the narcissist, whether it is a family gathering or an upcoming event, start thinking. What could happen or go wrong? You may be familiar with their predictable behavior and you can use that to your advantage. Come up with a plan on different scenarios that you may encounter. What triggers you and which action do they take that cripples you? Imagine it and take a deep breath. How could you respond and react in a healthier way? Thinking about a plan, or a way to cope and manage, can make you feel more prepared when the next encounter comes.

Oftentimes when others walk away or inflict hurt upon us, we are left questioning ourselves. We dissect every memory, moment, and action to search for answers of what went wrong. Our self worth begins to crumble. Sometimes when a toxic person hurts you, it's because they are bringing you down in order to justify their actions. People don't like to own up to their mistakes or take responsibility for their actions, and they get away with it by adding insult to injury. While you are feeling blindsided, broken, or down, they get you to believe that it is all your fault. Just remember that you are going to get through this and you will look back and appreciate your growth and outcome, as hard as it may be to see now.

As much as you may wish to have a healthy relationship with someone, it does not mean that person is capable of giving that. Whether it is a family member or friend, we always hope for a mutually respectful and harmonious relationship. It can be frustrating when it doesn't work out that way. We have no control over other people's actions. We can still grieve what we can't have, as it doesn't always mean the relationship was not wanted. Sometimes, it was very much wanted. It may be time to accept that someone is not capable of meeting your needs, and may never be. It is okay to put space between yourself and someone you love.

EIGHT

Toxic Positivity

"And if you complain once more
You'll meet an army of me"
-Army of Me by Björk

M any of us were raised to suck it up and smile. Well, fuck that. I want my friends and family to be real. I want to know about your shitty day. We all have those days. I want authenticity. Raw. I don't want you to fake anything for me or anyone else. Let people feel safe. Break the stigma of bottling everything up and giving autopilot responses like "I'm fine, and you?" Mental health is an epidemic because we all participate in hiding, thus making people feel alone. It's time for change.

We are programmed to praise positivity and joy while shunning grief and sadness, which isolates those who need help. As children grow up after years of being told to behave and smile, they become adults wearing masks. Our bodies suppress anger, pain, sorrow, suffering, and negative emotions that we are not allowed to acknowledge. These buried feelings grow with no release as we walk rampant, showing our teeth to the world to presume only happiness exists within us.

Relationships deepen through vulnerability. People need to open up about their fears, not tuck them away to pretend life is perfect. The world sees strength defined as being tough and resistant to anything other than joy. Sensitivity is seen as a weakness.

People need to open up about their sorrows, not hide them with a smile that says "I'm fine." People need to discuss their anger, not bottle it up. People will explode. People will crumble. How can anyone heal in an environment that doesn't allow basic human emotion to be released? Positivity and denial can look very similar. We are so wrapped up in a world of staying positive that we are ashamed to feel anything else.

We are all responsible and need to change our mindset so that we can make others feel safe enough to talk and reach out. Our culture is designed to suppress half of our basic human emotions, leaving us depressed actors. It is time to face the reality that life is not perfect and human emotions are not linear. Life is hard and pretending that we are all okay is dangerously exhausting, and one by one people are giving up. Stop telling people to suck it up or that they will be fine. Ask how you can help, listen, and pay attention to the subtle details. Check on your strong friends, your happy friends, and your quiet friends.

Take off your masks and let others know it's okay to not be okay. It is okay to cry, to grieve, to be angry, to feel lost and to feel frustrated. We are not robots. We can't heal by dreaming of rainbows to swallow our pain and trauma. We heal through a process. We prevent crumbling by expressing emotions. We cannot continue to build a stigma that negative emotions equal weakness. It is time to change the rules.

"Positive vibes only" equates to denial and refusal to acknowledge that strength and evolving grows from suffering and pain. Something I hear often is, "You're going to be okay." The reality is no one really knows if anyone will be okay. It's great to have a positive mindset but sometimes people get scared. Sometimes shit hits the fan and everything is not okay. So, what do you say instead of something dismissive like, "You'll be fine," and changing the subject. A more supportive and compassionate response would be, "How are you feeling?" or, "I am here if you need me."

You are allowed to feel, that's how you heal.

How to Be There for Someone with a Chronic Illness

Imagine you have two people who are not on the same page, let alone the same book. One struggles with chronic illness and the other is averagely healthy and maybe even deals with a common ailment here and there. How can they relate when it comes to health? It may not come easy to some when they have never had their health jeopardized. It is important to build a bridge to have a connection with your family or friends.

If you are the healthy one in this situation, perhaps you have a friend or loved one who has an invisible illness. This means that they look healthy on the outside but on the inside they struggle with an illness like diabetes, lupus, PTSD, POTS, thyroid diseases, cardiac and neurological diseases, to name a few. It can be tough to look at someone who looks fully capable of living life the way you do, but we are all different. Understand that just because you may be healthy and can juggle so many tasks, that does not mean it comes easy for others.

It is important to recognize that with all things, there is a spectrum. With chronic illnesses, that spectrum can vary day to day. One morning, we may have so much energy that we can clean the house and go out to get lunch, but the next morning we may be bedridden. Personally, putting on makeup every day is my way of putting on war paint. I hide my dark circles from waking up every hour. I conceal the redness in my face or sometimes add blush to my pale skin. When I look well, I don't get asked if I am sick or told I look tired. I feel normal and ready to take on the day.

Just because your friend or loved one looks put together and seems young and healthy, doesn't mean she or he wasn't up at 4:00 a.m. with severe back spasms and again at 5:00 a.m. feeling dehydrated, and once again at 6:00 a.m. in more pain until it is finally time to get up for the day. They probably got dizzy a few different times while their blood pressure dropped, causing nausea and tachycardia. Be grateful they answered the phone or showed up for lunch and they will be grateful for you.

How to Show Support to Your Disabled, Depressed, or Loved One:

- **Understanding** – Trying to understand what life is like for your friend or loved one shows a lot of compassion and empathy. This is your biggest step and the most important. For some, we are constantly judged, assumed we are lazy, told it is in our head, called a hypochondriac or just straight up dismissed. Many people are dismissive because they simply don't know what to say. Certain medical conditions sometimes take up to a decade or longer to get diagnosed. Oftentimes, there are several misdiagnoses and some people get left in a grey area where no one knows what to do. We feel alone and lost. We don't want sympathy, in fact it makes most of us uncomfortable. Compassion goes a long way.

- **Keep your ideals to yourself** – We appreciate your concerns, absolutely. I can vouch for myself that I have done plenty of research, am fully aware of my body and what is normal for me, have a strict diet with optimal nutrition and supplements, am a non-drinker, a non-smoker and I always try to look on the positive side as well as seeing a therapist when I can. My health is a full time job. You can't even pronounce what illnesses I have so please don't try to cure me. Of course, many of us appreciate advice but keep it simple and keep it at that. Do not try to push your ideals on someone or tell them if they exercise more they will feel better or that they can meditate to a cure. All we want is a shoulder to cry on, a listening ear, love and understanding.

- **If you are sick, stay the fuck away!** – Some of us have compromised immune systems and if you have a cold or flu and bring your germs to anyone, even a healthy person, it is just simply rude. If you bring your germs to someone who is already ill, it is cruel. We don't fight infections and other illnesses very well and most of the time it makes our other issues worse and for some, it could mean a trip to the hospital. I say this pre-COVID, as I used to get exposed to seasonal illnesses regularly when I worked in the salon. I can only hope that in the post-pandemic era this is a given.

- **Social gatherings** – There is a good chance we might not make it to your event or night out. I can assure you that we wish we were there but more often than not, our health makes us flakey friends. Please don't stop inviting us! We will always try, even if the chances are slim. Also, please don't get upset with us if we don't make it. We would rather be out having fun with you than stuck in bed.

- **Know that we are fighting a battle** – If we seem a little off, let us be a little off. There have been countless times when I was hanging out with someone when my vision blurred and I started seeing stars, getting light headed and having heart palpitations, but I pushed through it because that is my normal life. Something that has always bothered me was when strangers, coworkers or peers said, "Smile! It can't be that bad!" Well, maybe I was struggling with an ocular migraine that day, low blood pressure or didn't sleep well, so if I have a case of resting bitch face then let it be. I know it could always be worse but I am here, smile or not!

- **My illness does not define me** – I am a strong warrior. I love art, music, travel, culture, anything vintage, food, nature, giving back and being creative. I can be sensitive but I persevere and I keep my chin up. I have not given up and I won't. I have bad days but I climb above it and stay positive, even if it is a full time job. I am not my illness. However, it is part of my life, whether big or small. It may affect me but it is not who I am.

- **Don't ask an open-ended question in regards to helping out** – An example is asking someone if there is anything you can do to help; this is too broad of an offer. Though it is very kind, most likely the person you offered help to will feel too embarrassed to think of a specific thing. Instead, offer specific help, such as a housecleaning or dropping off dinner on an assigned night. Not only is this assistance incredibly helpful, but you also surpassed the uneasy ice breaker. No one knows what scope of help you are willing to give, nor do they want to feel like they might be asking too much. So, if you truly want your assistance redeemed, then don't give them the option to think and ask… just tell them when and how.

- **Let us vent** – You don't need to have any answers or advice, just listen. We are used to small talk and the autopilot response, "I am fine, and you?" Advice is usually not something we are looking for unless we ask. Oftentimes, we become victims online to sales pitches to cure our illnesses. Some of us are vulnerable and desperate while others are over it. It is likely we are very familiar with our health and have been living with chronic illnesses for some time. We tend to research, educate and advocate for our health. However, if we don't feel like talking about it, then just being present and distracting us from our health is a nice break. When we do want to open up and vent about our health, just listen.

- **We are not lazy** – "It must be nice to be in bed all day," is going to get you the asshole award. Trust me, we would rather have an adventurous life or be out at the beach, out with friends, hustling our dream career, or working on a fun project, but instead we are prisoners to our own body. Be mindful that spending the day in bed is not as glorious as it sounds for a chronically ill person.

- **"You don't look sick"** – or "you are too young and healthy to be sick," is something that we hear often, and it only shows ignorance and a lack of empathy. Invisible illnesses are not obvious or blatantly apparent and because of this, we are often dismissed by medical professionals or deemed drug seekers. When you say that, it feels like a betrayal and a reminder that no one understands. We may post our good day selfies or fun outings but what you don't see is the 24/7 pain, depression and grieving, the tears, the complications, and multiple doctor visits. You see a mask, warrior paint and the fake normal version of ourselves. We just hide it well.

- **Gift suggestions** – I bring this topic up as many people over the years have reached out to me, asking for suggestions for a friend or loved one in the hospital. Since I am a frequent flyer at the hospital, I seemed to have learned what to pack, if I get that luxury. If we are in the hospital or recovering from surgery, there are many little gift suggestions. Here are some great go-to items: face wipes, lip balm, books, magazines, fuzzy blanket, fuzzy socks, essential oils, snacks, headphones, a notebook or journal. For post-hospital suggestions: gift cards for meal deliveries, food, grocery store run, house cleaning, or baby sitting. Try to give warnings before stopping by so that we have a moment to prepare. Many of us have diet restrictions, so it is always good to ask.

- **Patience** – We feel guilt and a whirlwind of emotions for having a chronic illness and for anyone who is involved. Some of us are still recovering from the trauma of medical gaslighting or loved ones who don't believe us. I know I felt like a burden and still occasionally have to stop those thoughts. Your patience and support mean the world to us, even if we have a hard time showing it. Don't be afraid to point out our flaws, but please try to be understanding and forgiving, as sometimes we don't realize our suffering is showing in ways that can affect you, like an attitude or resting bitch face. Just tell us it's okay and help us through, instead of getting angry.

- **Space** – Friends aren't supposed to abandon you during the hardest times of your life, but some do. When you choose to give someone space, it's not for them, it's for you and your own discomfort on how to respond or handle what's going on. If someone wants space, they will either tell you or not answer your calls. Everytime I have a major event in my life, people decided to give me space. These were during the most difficult times in my life, when the last thing I needed was space. Even if I couldn't talk, or didn't want to, it was comforting to know I had support or people checking in on me. The ones who show up are usually those who have been through it too. They understand the grief and heartache. Or, they are very intuitive and empathic. I will forever remember those who were there at my worst.

- **Imagine.** I hope you never understand the feeling of living with an incurable disease. Knowing there isn't a cure for my illness is a feeling I would not wish on anyone.

Many people will not understand this, and if you are that person, consider yourself lucky. Recall the last time you were under the weather, and ask yourself how you would handle that feeling forever.

You Got This!

During a crisis, traumatic event, an uphill battle, or any stressful situation, many people are programmed to respond with a motivational poster-type quote like, "Hang in there," or, "You got this!" Social workers are trained to just listen, and even if they respond with a "Wow," they don't say it is going to be okay or that they know what you are going through. The truth is, we never really know if we will be okay. Sometimes we aren't okay. We also never really know what someone is going through because there are other variables involved and different histories and past traumas to consider. Everyone is individually unique in their journey of life. It isn't a pissing contest either. Don't compare how you handled something to another person. We are all at our own speed and it's not a race. Just lend a hand or an ear.

Instead of saying, "You are going to be fine," try offering help or just listen. There is a difference between hearing and listening. You can hear someone talk, but are you listening? Some people just need to vent--it's how they process and unpack their emotional baggage. Some people just want to feel heard.

If you are the person who needs to vent, know your audience. Your friends or loved ones can't always give you what you need. They are not licensed professionals after all. If they aren't offering support, be transparent. Let them know it bothers you that you can't be real with them, that you don't want some positive bullshit quote. Let them know that you aren't looking for a solution, but just to be heard.

NINE

Poems

*"Mirror, mirror on the wall
What's the meaning of it all?"*
Kids These Days - Shakey Graves

I have written as an outlet since I was in my teens. My first saved poem that I could find was from the age of 15. As you read through my poems, you will notice how lost and broken I was. Some were hard to read and difficult to share. I was so deeply depressed and in my own dark, isolated world. I never want anyone to feel the way I did. The reason I am called to share my writing is because I want others to see how hopeless I felt, yet how strong I feel now. There is hope and there is light--you just have to find it and be willing and open to see it.

The Birth and Death of Love and Lust (1999)

My veins rotting with lust and taunting desire.
My heart, unfiltered, pumping pungent incurable passion.
Devouring every molecule of my flesh,
Like a drug dragging through my blood.
Conceiving thoughts of your soft lips trickling down my neck.
Our legs tangled together.
Our hearts racing like hummingbirds.
Feverish face turning pink,
breathing as if each breath were my first.

We have become but only rotten fruit,
To the touch we fall apart.
No reviving.
No resurrection.
Just a mess of desolate decaying matter that was
Once a fresh ripe
Savory decadent ecstasy.

Now there lies our dead weary plod of unity
Like a corpse under the floorboard.
A nervous havoc.
The stench of our dead future still
Haunts me as I crawl into my cold empty bed
Where once your warm body welcomed me.

Indulgence of your venom.
My heart seems to ache for you, to be an empty vessel
Yet I can see the gleaming end of this murky tunnel.
But still look in the other direction in disbelief.
Compulsively tormenting myself.

POEMS

Missouri

A sting on my leg: an ant.
I press my finger over its body and smash its existence.

My bare feet run over the sharp grass,
occasionally catching a rock.
They are dirty and rough, unlike most little girls.

I sit inside of a pretend home built from bushes and trees.
It is quiet and I imagine this is my castle.

I walk around my pretend castle,
stepping on wild strawberries.
Is that blood on my toes from the rocks and thorns,
or just a smashed berry?
Sometimes it's both.

GARDEN OF BLU

Repeat (2013)

Lonely girl who stares down an empty glass

Barefoot, stuck at home, and sitting on her ass

Dreams too big to swallow
So she closes her eyes until tomorrow

POEMS

Wilt (2007)

Misti Blu, swallowed by the sea
She had a heart but there was no key

Even the sunniest days were dark
Daydreaming for a little spark

Living in a state of vacancy
Under a violent sky of complacency

Her heart too big to function,
Leaving her life in a constant state of dysfunction

Indecision

If I turn left, the dewy grass cools my feet.
Warm sun kisses my skin.
Picking berries until my fingers stain blood red.
Sweet warm sun and solitude.

If I turn right,
the dark velvet sky turns city lights into fireflies.
Cool breezes dance through my hair.
Moonlit adventures until my eyes collapse.
When I sleep, I dream.

Dusk or dawn, when black and white turn grey.
Do you turn left, right, or do you stay?

The Dark Cloud

A feeling grows over you, nuzzling into the pit of your stomach that buzzes out to your limbs. It's like you are standing at the edge of a cliff but there is no beautiful view, just a worry so strong that it consumes you. Your blood feels thick as it boils through your veins, dragging it's gloom to the surface of your skin, begging to get out. This is the feeling that takes over your brain, your gut and your heart. It's the aftershock of a traumatic event that creeps up on you, tapping you on the shoulder and pouring itself into your bones.

Brain Storm (2013)

My naked body lies in the porcelain white tub. Knees up and head on the hard cold bottom. Staring up at the window, the steam from the hot water blurs the outside world. Hot water crawls up my back and reaches my neck while my hair delicately dances on the surface of the bath water. My skin turns pink from the hot bath while the water gently swallows me. The sound of the faucet water filling the tub slowly muffles then disappears as it creeps inside my ears. I stare at the white ceiling, taking shallow breaths. The thoughts swirling in my mind are for once quiet and numb. The water seeps into the sides of my lips and in my mouth. My eyes fill with the hot burning water and now not only can I not hear, but I can't see. Shallow breaths out of my damp nostrils, soon I wouldn't breathe. Just as the water slides down my nose, burning the back of my throat, I slide my foot over to the plug and pull it. Slowly my sight comes back and I can hear the water being sucked down the drain along with my heart. I watch the condensation on the window roll down like tears and I get up. I stare at the foggy mirror, where my reflection would be, watching as the steam slowly disappears and I can see myself again.

Wine to Whiskey

*The first time I took communion I watched as an elderly
woman beside me got on her knees and held her delicate
hands out, eyes closed, her skin like paper; the sinful blood
flowing through her veins looked blue. I knelt down next to
her, my warm bare knees sticking to the pew. I held out my
hands and closed my eyes enough to look like I knew what
I was doing but opened just enough to see what I should do
next. The woman parted her lips and took in the body of
Christ. Her lips were a cheap pink, leaving residue on the
glass that wasn't fully wiped away.*
*I felt so small holding this large glass,
the blood of Christ in my hands.*
The wine burned my throat all the way down into my belly.

Loose Change

Pass around my heart like loose change. A little bit of your filth will remain on each penny. You'll drop a few dimes along the ride that will never be found again. You'll trade some quarters in for cigarettes and when you're down to your last nickel, you'll almost be done with me; soon there will be nothing left.

POEMS

Birdcage

My wings are clipped and I'm sitting here in a small cage
trying to make comfort out of my own shit

Shitting where I sleep

Slowly losing sight of the horizon
while I rot in this cookie cutter town

Colors on my feathers fade

Time Travel (2008)

Staring at a photograph of myself in my early teens: long blonde hair, a cross necklace. I was innocent. I was sweet. I was full of hope. Then, I look at myself now. I won't step foot in a church. I chopped off my long pretty, blonde locks and colored my hair a black noir. I've made a lot of mistakes. I've broken a few hearts. I've done everything I said I would never do. I can't help but stare at that girl, and the girl I am now and wonder how they could be the same person, pumping the same blood through the same heart. I can't help but think about that girl, buried and gone. I am but only the weeds growing out of her, growing and forming into nothing but a plant to be ripped up and tossed away.

Hunting a Hunter (2008)

It wasn't you I couldn't let go of. It was me. I was just like you. I was always going to run the other way too. I was always going to slither away without trying to wake anyone. I was always going to be unattainable. I wasn't the cat. I'm the mouse who runs. Not the hunter, but the prey who runs for dear life.

GARDEN OF BLU

Wet Blanket

Something about the way the moonlight cloaks the murky water, reflecting the stars that we wish upon and veiling the caliginous soul of the earth.

POEMS

Fortress

Surrender your heart

Glass Lamp

Sometimes she shines bright, other times she is lost in the dark. When she glows, she lights the way for others: saving people from falling in the dark, to see what is in front of them, to illuminate life. But, in just a moment she can burn out and be just as lost in the dark as others.

When the sun shines through the windows, she feels useless. As she collects dust over the next few weeks, she feels neglected and unappreciated. Sometimes she is unplugged while something else gets more use. And just like that, one wrong move and she falls to the floor and shatters.

Remains

Desolate dismay, buried deep in our hearts like mosquitoes trapped in amber, beautifully and permanently encased. The vast sea of the mind will always have veiled shadows.

Invisible Illness

A world gone blind
It's all in your mind

There isn't a sign
You must be fine

What I cannot see
Must not be

You're not dying
So you must be lying

POEMS

Moonflower

She was tired,
It was how she was wired.
She fought
For everything she sought.
She was brave
While she rode each wave.
And when the world felt like doom,
She would still bloom.

Reflection

Are you still there?
Bad days turn into weeks
Strengths are suffocating
Dreams are drifting
Nothing seems fair
Tears turn into fears
Don't get lost
You are more than your flaws
Don't drown in your limitations
Don't give up
You have a purpose
I still see you

POEMS

When I'm Gone

One day, when I am just a memory
In your heart you will carry me
Forever with you, I will be
A part of you and with thee

Shark Week

Tuesday.

Like clockwork, the darkness would smother me like a thick velvet blanket.

"This will pass. Just get through this."

I lie in bed. Pure silence. The light from the windows slowly dances around the room with each hour. The phone rings and dings as I stare at it, catatonically dismissing the need to see who is trying to reach me.

The light of the outside world slowly fades as the darkness of the night fills the room. I haven't moved.

My mind wanders and suddenly I catch my thoughts, realizing that I am imagining all of the ways I could end my life.

"Stop. Just get through these next few days."

I begin to feel hot. Thirsty. I don't want to move.

The evening turns into morning.

Wednesday.

I'm up. I move. I eat.

"Are you okay? Are you getting my texts?" I read my messages, answer them in my mind but don't feel like making the effort to respond. I can't. I lie back down and stare at the T.V. It's turned off. I stare at the blank screen in silence for hours.

My stomach rumbles. It's already evening.
A rush comes over me. I feel overwhelmed with grief, sadness,

anger, and pure doom. I pace a little bit, feeling the cold floor against my bare feet. It's 4:00 a.m.

I lie down. It's so dark that I can't tell the difference between my eyes being closed or open.

Thursday.

The sun pours through the window. The blue sky is calling my name. I go outside. I take a deep breath.

What should I do today?

I have twenty-six more days until the darkness returns.

TEN

Chasing Love

"Good times for a change
See, the luck I've had
Can make a good man
Turn bad"

-Please, Please, Please Let Me Get What I Want by The Smiths

Are You Coming To Bed? (2002)

Wearing an oversized shirt, your shirt, which vaguely your scent remains…. and a pair of small panties, the cute ones that you like. Barefoot, sleepy, and wanting you to crawl into bed with me, under our soft sheets. Pulling each other's bodies closer. Your pheromones, soft skin… your hand on my lower back pulling me towards your body. Hand sliding under my shirt. Our warm skin melts into one.

I want to wake up to morning breath and messy hair. I want to wake up without makeup and you think that I look more beautiful than ever. I want to wake up to you every morning for the rest of my life. I want to be in a framed photo on your office desk. I want to call you my husband. I want to look at you ten years later and just get the chills because it still feels like a dream.I want to meet you one day but I don't think you exist.

I'm not even sure if I believe in any of this. I'm content with being alone and definitely not looking for anyone, but sometimes I get lost thinking about it--about being in love. I wonder what it feels like having that.

Confetti (2006)

He tarnishes me. He rips me to shreds and throws me up in the air like confetti then complains about the mess.

Tetanus (2006)

My weathered heart has been through many storms. It only takes the smallest bit of rust to turn into fragile flaking beats. You can't give your whole heart then, just a little debris before it withers away into a pile of scrap.

Matador (2007)

The air that leaves your mouth, forming the sound of an apology, only becomes a lie that gets caught between your teeth. By now, your smile has become a filthy scene, in which I cannot bear to look at.
You are like a wild bull on the loose, ready to kill. Those cheering in the crowd are your encouraging thoughts. I am the bare red flag dangling in your view and with every fiber of your existence, you thirst for my demise.
As feeble as a red flag may look, only taking the gentlest of violence, it always outlives the bull.

Another Box to Collect Dust (2007)

I am strong and brave. My heart and soul are temporarily disabled. My heart was a canvas in which you've destroyed. I once was intelligent, beautiful, extroverted, tough, confident, and strong. I stood tall and I feared nothing. I protected my heart from the epitome of what you are. I did not give you my heart, you are a thief. You broke in and ripped me apart to nothing but a coward who fears everything in life, even life itself. You've turned me into a foolish, bitter, incompetent, worthless human being that doesn't deserve anything in this world but a spot in hell. I have doubted myself for so long. I have hated myself to a point of numbness and self destruction. I have lost every and any bit of hope. Every fiber or molecule of passion is gone.

Sometimes it takes a cool breeze and a sorbet sunset to get lost in and see the light again. Sometimes it takes a child's laugh or chance of a fresh start, legal safety, or boxes, to get a hint or taste of what the future could hold. Sometimes it takes getting lost in what color I'd paint my new walls. Then, like cancer it grows, multiplying. One cell of strength or hope breeding and then soon taking over the emptiness. And then soon I'd notice I'm standing tall, I'm brave. There is an answer to everything. A smile on my face--I am smart, beautiful, and strong, and nothing or nobody can ever, ever take that away. Ever.

Crumbs (2010)

*We are the crumbs under the toaster that everyone neglects
to clean. We are the weeds that grow in the cracks of the
sidewalks that no one gets rid of. We are the ugly sweater that
your grandmother gave you, collecting dust in the back of
your closet (you will never wear it but you keep it anyway).
We are the one bad song that everyone skips.
You think love is sweet, then the ants come.*

Two Way Mirror (2013)

At one point, someone had made your heart swell and eyes sparkle, while now the very same person makes you feel empty and your eyes fill with sorrow. Or, someone can easily wander in and break a home, and for that small instantly gratifying moment, they dismiss all their blood, sweat and tears for a small taste that will burn an entire home down. We shed tears and then easily laugh later. Lust turns into disgust. Everything and everyone seems so interchangeable, replaceable, and temporary—yet we keep running on the hamster wheel trying to get somewhere.

Cup of Joe (2014)

A life with me is like playing house. I am just a mask, to feel grown up. I am not the dream, but warm arms for you to later slip out of with dismay. If I were a strange girl, you would show me all your best moves, pour my glass of whiskey first like you used to. Instead, you take me from behind so you can use your imagination, or take your rough hands into the bathroom while I am away. I am not the fantasy but just a comfortable place to rest your callused feet while I cut up your steak, filling your belly and mending your wounds until you muster up the energy to seek a more fruitful option. I am what you settle for when your hairline recedes and your dreams fail.

Belly Ache (2014)

Nomad Romeo, making wishes that won't come true. Always hungry but I have nothing you crave. Keep searching for something to soothe your hunger pangs.
Sweetness will rot your teeth.

Future Holds the Hand of the Past

Who you are today is shaped by your past and how you allowed your past to transform you.

Ask yourself: is your perspective the only reality? People tend to forget that there is more to every story. Some lines in a chapter are skipped over, blurry, or perhaps we were distracted, forgot, or misread. How accurate are your memories? Were you clear minded at the time? Have you grown since or changed your mindset? When you think shitty thoughts about yourself, you attract shitty people and exist in a shitty environment. When you grow and think of yourself as constantly blooming, you will attract people who are also healing and blooming, thus thriving in a blossoming environment. It took me such a long time to raise my standards, not only for myself but for those I allowed into my life. This is why it is important to know your worth.

As I look back at the relationships throughout my life, I recall the many stages of growth I experienced. I went from wanting a fairytale and upheaving unrealistic expectations onto unequipped partners, to being bitter, destructive, and cold in order to subconsciously protect my heart. I would run, hit the destruct button and never look back. It was my way of avoiding getting hurt, but by doing so I hurt others. Then, I began to slide back into seeking a healthy, mature relationship. I was not able to come anywhere close to that until I did some major, deep self-healing. Even when I thought I learned my self-worth, I still had moments of fear, flashbacks and triggers into the past that had me sliding backwards. When that happened, I would acknowledge my mistakes, dig into what provoked my behavior, and work through it. I would learn and keep trying. I would continue to grow.

If you are in a relationship or not, you can't expect one person to make you happy and fulfill every aspect of your needs. We have family, friends, and therapists for that. If you pile your expectations onto one individual, they will not always be able to carry everything, or at least not well. Resentment builds and relationships crumble. If you want roses on Valentine's Day but know that no one will be getting them for you, treat yourself.

Kissing Girls

I grew up like most little girls, playing with barbies and cooking in my miniature kitchen. I would carry around my plastic baby, wrapped in a pink fuzzy blanket, and I would tuck her in at night. At such a young age, we are raised to fit into gender roles based on the toys available for our gender. I really did love playing with barbies and creating a dramatic soap opera of a story between the dolls. I loved unicorns and for a moment, I even wanted to be a fashion designer. My mom was never into the typical feminine styles. She rode a motorcycle and had tattoos. If she wore makeup, it was eyeliner and mascara. I grew up with an older brother so as much as I played with dolls, GI Joes were included. I also loved to go camping and pretend to be a Kung Fu fighter. I played video games and farted back at the boys as we would laugh and out-fart each other. I never knew how to use a blow dryer until I learned how to in cosmetology school. I first waxed my eyebrows my freshman year in high school after a girl told me that my eyebrows looked like beavers on my face.

In junior high, I was so close with my best friend that people would tease us and call us lesbians. My first encounter with that word was directed as an insult. I remember feeling hurt and embarrassed. This word was meant to hurt and embarrass us and it did. At this age, I was still not quite interested in the idea of sex. Anything sexual at this point in my life was only about the feeling I could achieve by myself. I wasn't thinking about someone. I wasn't fantasizing. If anything, I was struggling with the idea that I was sinning and going to hell for even thinking about sex. I had no interest in kissing anyone. There I was being teased about something I hadn't even thought of yet.

I was supposed to like boys, so I did. I remember the first time I kissed a girl. I was a teenager and it was a dare. Our boyfriends laughed at us as we kissed and yet we continued to kiss until they became uncomfortable. Her boyfriend left the room upset. I spent most of my twenties kissing girls but still dating men. Usually after every breakup I would hook up with a woman. I wanted to date women, but where I lived there were only a small handful of options and it just never worked out. Despite my long history of an obvious attraction to women, I never called myself bisexual. I know my family would accept me if I had developed a substantial relationship with a woman, but I still kept this part of myself "in the closet."

Having a daughter of my own, I have learned that equality is still a struggle as sexuality remains on the frontline of personal rights. Young girls and boys still feel scared to come out. People still shun their loved one when they come out. I have never been attracted to someone based on how they look. I have always been attracted to the connection with the person, and how they make me feel. I am happily married to a man who loves me and tells me every morning as he leaves for work that I am his world. Even though this may be irrelevant personally, I feel called to finally expose part of myself that I have always hid. I want to share this for those who feel unaccepted, scared, or alone: *I am bisexual.*

Butterfly

You go through so many transformations throughout your life, that some versions of yourself are complete strangers. No matter what type of relationships you have, in time people will change. Your people are the ones who love you as you transform throughout life. They appreciate how you bloom, even during the ugliness of the process. We all have seasons, whether dark or bright, warm or cold. We morph as we grow and sometimes we fall into a slump or get a little lost. Not everyone has known the best version of you, the healed version, or the broken version. Not everyone sees the whole picture or your evolving growth. Those are the ones you keep around, not the ones who only love you at your best.

Love Story

When I met my husband, it wasn't the right time. It was not the right time for a couple of years, and I honestly thought it was never going to happen at that point. We were never single at the same time and the stars hadn't aligned…yet. I was in a much better place in my life, but the universe was testing me with another shitty boyfriend. I started seeing the signs, noticing the lies, and finding clues. I was about to break up with him, as I collected enough evidence to learn that he was a pathological liar who was taking advantage of me and hiding the fact that he liked to pop pills. Suddenly, I get a message from my future husband asking if I'd like to meet up.

OMG! Holy shit.

Well, I had to decline but we started talking more. However, he was single and I was not. He showed up at a restaurant I bartended for at the time. I was so nervous that my hands were shaking, so I tossed the menu in front of him so he wouldn't catch on. We smiled and flirted. He finished his food and left. Soon after, he asked me out again. I told him to give me a week, explaining my situation, and then I broke up with the guy I was seeing.

My husband and I have been inseparable ever since. Everything moved fast but there were no red flags for me to swat away and ignore. There were just NO RED FLAGS! Our love was so easy and comfortable, but I still struggled with feeling insecure. I knew I didn't want to sabotage our relationship by letting fear take over, so I started seeing a therapist.

Relationships are hard work, even when they are easy. I chose to put in the effort and to see a therapist to work through my fears and issues. It was not fair to my husband to be penalized for the damage done by people who were in my life before he was. He couldn't wait to meet my kids and they accepted him and loved him right away. It never felt like an obligation, like my past relationships. When he was ready to propose, he asked my children for permission.

We were only engaged for a few months at the time, but my health was continuing to deteriorate. I had been in and out of emergency rooms and sometimes taken by ambulance. My heart was going into serious arrhythmias and I was afraid for my life. Several times I told him that I loved him, worried it would be the last. I finally got my pacemaker, and three weeks later we decided to elope. He didn't want to be the boyfriend stuck in the waiting room, he wanted to be my husband at my side. We knew how much we cared for each other, as tomorrow was not promised. Our time was precious and valuable.

How to Fight

Falling in love is easy and exhilarating. Conflict is inevitable in any relationship. The good times are simple to navigate, but where most people struggle is how to fight. When two people who love each other have a disagreement or turmoil, it can be detrimental and earth-shattering. Learning to communicate, setting and respecting boundaries, giving space to cool down, and hearing the other side are a few key points to working through a fight.

We all have our baggage stuffed full of our past traumas that contribute to the way we behave and respond. In the beginning, my husband and I sucked at fighting. Over time, we learned each other's triggers and learned how we prefer to deal with our conflicts. We continue to choose to make the effort to build the foundation of our relationship. We work on our own personal growth and continue to strengthen our marriage. It still drives me crazy that he throws his clothes on the floor next to the laundry basket, and I'm sure he isn't a fan of my much needed alone time, but I love our love.

I often see people post on social media groups, complaining about their significant others: not being believed about their illness, not being supported, and being called names. I know I have been there before, but it breaks my heart to see people stay in a toxic relationship because they don't want to be alone. There is no shame in being alone; it is the best time to get to know yourself and to work on your goals. If someone is not willing to grow with you, pluck that weed and move on.

ELEVEN

Mama Tried

"Back then, I didn't know why
Why you were misunderstood
So now, I see through your eyes
All that you did was love"
-Mama by Spice Girls

O ur parents raised us while they were still trying to figure out life themselves. After we leave the nest, we flounder about and find ways to heal and cope with the life we have been given. Generational trauma spills over onto the next, as cycles morph from each compensation. For example, my generation grew up on the loose. We had no cell phones during childhood. We just had to be back by dark. We did stupid things and somehow managed to live through it. Now, as parents ourselves, many compensate for their upbringing by being overly involved and tracking their child's every move (because of what we ourselves were capable of). Next, our children will raise their children a particular way, thus compensating for having no privacy and freedom. Our children's lives have been shared online to the masses, every detail, from diaper rashes to graduation.

Groundhog Day

I didn't always want to be a mother. When I was sixteen, my heart was set on living out of a suitcase, while traveling the world as a nomadic artist and photographer. I think the universe had a way of grounding me by sprinkling children into my life at a young age. Had it not been for them, who knows where I would be or who I would have become. I was always so lost but having kids gave me a light to follow and a reason to hold on.

When I was seventeen, I still hadn't been in a relationship that lasted longer than an awkward few weeks. I had crushes and dated a few guys for short stints. I was usually dumped after they found out I was a virgin and that they weren't going to be the one. They would break up with me and go for a girl who was already having sex or liked to party. I didn't have breasts until high school, so that didn't help either. Everyone was interested in smoking, drinking, and hooking up, while I was trying to find the meaning of life.

I moved to Florida from Missouri at the age of sixteen, but I was always the youngest in my grade. It was in the middle of my junior year and I made a few friends. I was working at a pizza place in Cocoa Village. It was Mardi Gras in the village where I worked and I was selling slices of pizza to the masses, then hanging out with friends after. I remember wearing a white crop top, navy baggy pants with a seatbelt belt. It was around March of 2002. A guy that was twice my age kept putting his hands on me, calling me sweetie, and saying he was going to take me home. My friends came up to the pizza place to see if I was done working. They had a friend with them that I had never met. The older guy continued to come onto me so I walked over and wrapped my arms around the new friend and whispered, "Just play along." I introduced him to the creep as my boyfriend. He walked away and we all ran off to hang out for the night.

I introduced myself to my pretend boyfriend and apologized, explaining the situation. He told me he didn't mind and we continued seeing each other after that. He was not my first love or the one, but he was there at the right time. It was a time in my life where I didn't want to be called "the ice princess" or "the virgin" anymore. I saw all my friends having boyfriends and I hung out with couples. I couldn't relate to their sex lives or dramatic relationships and I finally wanted to. I wanted that excitement and drama. He was the one who I was going to be with. I was finally ready and nearly eighteen.

I remember seeing a tarot card reader for the first time, just as our relationship began. He was with me and the tarot card reader told him to wait outside. She instantly informed me that he was "bad for me" and that we would not last. I was already frustrated and we hadn't even begun. She pulled the ten of cups card, a couple with children that appeared to be happy. In my mind I thought this woman was crazy. She didn't know me or know that I had plans to be childless and wandering Amsterdam as I became a famous artist. I left feeling scammed.

When I was with him, I got lost in the idea of him being the only one. I wanted the fairytale of falling in love and being with one person for the rest of my life. I wanted perfection. This guy was a high school dropout and his parents were never present in his upbringing. I was blindly building a story in my head that clouded reality. In my mind, he was my prince charming. We were going to get married, have kids, and move away. Only, he didn't see the same story I saw. He was never going to save money. He was still seeing other girls on the side and he was never going to move away with me or be the person I made up in my mind. I already had a closet filled with appliances and savings to move out, and he couldn't hold onto a paycheck for longer than 24 hours.

Soon, I was pregnant. I was scared but excited because I was happy with the idea of marriage, kids, and having my own family different from how I was raised. I was barely eighteen when I found out and so was he. His reaction was to sleep with other girls, call out of work, and to go to parties. One night I called his workplace to ask him to pick something up from the store, like pancake cravings. They informed me that he never showed up that night and I paced around my room in tears, wondering where he was. Week after week he would do this and come home after midnight, with alcohol on his breath and bloodshot eyes. I would ask how work was and he would lie and say it was busy. I would pack his stuff and put it outside at least once a month. He always claimed that he was just getting it out of his system. Why couldn't he just be who I wanted him to be?

My first ultrasound was to see how far along I was. I was on and off so many birth control medications to regulate my period due to severe endometriosis. Birth control made me sick, so I came in often to try another brand. At one check up they informed me I was pregnant. Because the birth control made everything so irregular, they had to see how far along I was with an ultrasound. My mother came with me to the appointment. She was already quite shocked to begin with, but not as shocked as the technician who ran out of the room. The tech brought a doctor in to show him something. "Yes, just continue and tell them," the doctor said to the tech. The nervous new technician said, "I'm sorry, I just haven't seen this yet so I wanted to make sure."

I was so scared and asked, "Is there something wrong with my baby?"

"No," she said, "here is Baby A and here is Baby B." Our jaws dropped as we realized there were two babies. Twins!

❊ ❊ ❊

At only 20 weeks, I was two centimeters dilated. I was rushed to the hospital with my bed slanted nearly upside down to keep the pressure off my cervix. The hospital was almost an hour away and they were going 90 miles per hour. I was so scared. I loved my twin boys more than anything and I could not lose them. I was at the hospital for two weeks on strict bed rest and sent home just before Christmas. I continued to be on bed rest for weeks without changes. At my next check up, two weeks after coming home, I was four centimeters dilated. I was rushed back to the hospital just like before but only this time, I was staying. I managed to make it four more weeks. At 28 weeks, I had a nurse check me again, since it had been four weeks. She said I was 5 centimeters. I never knew at the time, but I was allergic to latex and that was what hospitals used then. Each time they examined me, I would dilate more.

I had spicy food from the hospital for lunch. I had been there for weeks and the twins' father came to visit sometimes but I tried not to think about what he was doing while I was chained to an IV in a hospital room. My stomach was killing me and I was having cramps from the food, or so I thought. I was on the toilet, pushing, and the nurse called the doctor after I requested medicine for my upset stomach.

"Get off the toilet!" My doctor barged in, "Now! Don't make me pull you off!"

"But I am going to the bathroom," I explained, confused as to why she thought it was acceptable to barge in on me like that. I was pooping!

"You are in labor and you are going to push them out into the toilet! You have 5 seconds to get off that toilet before I remove you myself."

I panicked and got up, walking to my bed in pain with what I thought were typical IBS cramps. I called the twins' father and my parents, telling them to hurry. Nurses flooded in and they wheeled me off to the operating room. I planned for a c-section due to my heart issues and having multiples. Everything happened so fast. I heard my babies cry and kissed their noses and just like that, they were taken away to the NICU.

I went into labor on February 1st, 2003 and they were born on the 2nd in the early morning. My parents had rushed over to Orlando, an hour drive. When I woke up, the nurses were crying. I thought the worst. The nurse handed me the newspaper and the headline was "Space Shuttle Columbia Disaster" where seven crew members were killed. I felt guilty to be relieved that my babies were okay, even though the doctor explained they had a 50% chance of survival. They were less than three pounds. Every day was touch and go. They were in the hospital for fifty-two days.

They came home still weighing under five pounds with oxygen and apnea monitors. They were on several medications every four hours, and had several specialists to follow up with. I had to measure and track their feedings and diaper changes. When they stopped breathing, an alarm would go off and this happened often. I would watch them turn blue while rubbing their chest and telling them to breathe. They ended up back in the hospital shortly after coming home. I never slept. There was no time to sleep while playing nurse 24/7 or fearing that my babies would stop breathing.

Everything was scary and parenting was structural and clinical rather than bonding and having these precious memories. I felt envious of other moms who had a supportive husband and their only struggle was finding a cute outfit to wear for photos. The twins were still fighting for their lives, seeing neurologists, cardiologists, ophthalmologists, pulmonologists, and so on. We were in and out of hospitals. Luckily, around eight months, they finally had their apnea monitors, medications, and oxygen removed. They were now able to be normal little babies that weren't attached to devices. But it was still terrifying not having an alarm. I would stand over them at night, staring at their chests and feeling for breaths. I didn't have time to acknowledge or address postpartum depression or the PTSD of being a mother of NICU babies.

My parents helped me and eventually, I finally kicked their father out. He never made the effort to step up or be involved. He barely made it to their birth. At one point, I was getting threats from him, his friends, and the girls he would date, so eventually I got a restraining order. He was in and out of jail and further and further away from our lives, until he just became a slight memory. He fully signed over his rights when the twins were five years old.

Letter From a Mother

Being a mother is carrying a tiny human being in your body for nine months while your flat stomach and perky breasts morph into something you could never imagine. It's uncomfortable and emotional from this point on. You become a snot rag and a sleep deprived superhero. All of this happens while juggling a career, relationships and putting yourself on the back burner for years to come.

Being a mother is staying up late to wash that third load of laundry and right when you start to drift into slumber, you hear your baby waking up. It means pausing the movie you are watching 37 times. When you are sick with a fever and vomiting, but you have to suck it up and keep going. There are no days off. If you work, coming home after a long day means a speedy trip to the grocery story before picking up the kids and flinging pots onto the stove.

While you cook dinner, laundry gets started and math questions you haven't seen in over a decade fog your memory. You secretly google on your phone "how to find the volume of a rectangular prism" and turn down the stovetop because something is starting to burn. Occasionally you pick at food, barbarically shoveling it into your mouth over the kitchen sink. You get one kid into the shower after telling them for the fourth time. You finally sneak away to undo the bra that has been cutting into your skin since 6:00 a.m. Finally, you get a brief moment to use the bathroom after holding it since after lunchtime and someone knocks on the door asking if dinner is ready. Fuck. You also just realized you forgot to call someone back and also forgot to pick up toilet paper at the store. You are always last to shower and right when it's time to rinse your hair, the water turns cold.

Being a mother means constantly drilling the meaning of life, good morals, lessons, and long talks in hopes that your children grow up to be healthy, happy, and well rounded human beings. It also means getting the eye roll, slammed door, whispering not so sweet nothings under their breath as they walk away with blatant disregard for all that you do. Your stomach is filled with worry each time they get sick or hurt. Your heart breaks into two when they get dissed by their first crush at school. You contemplate jail time when you hear about someone else's kid being mean to yours. You have to be the asshole right before report cards come out.

Being a mother is a thankless job. It's being the bad guy, making your children eat vegetables and convincing them to go to bed on time. It's telling them no when their father tells them yes and you have to deal with the aftermath of a sick or moody kid. It's a job where you always get criticized and a neverending filing cabinet of complaints. With your spare time, you work and pay bills, balance a chaotic schedule, and run to the bank and grocery store several times a week while trying not to leave the house with your shirt inside out.

When you walk into your messy home that you just cleaned the night before, dying to get comfortable and sit down, someone is already mad at you for your dinner selection and the toilet is clogged. Oh, there is a school project due in the morning that you never heard about, and we are out of cat food.

Motherhood: we do it and we do it well, with a smile and lots of concealer. We are tired and sometimes feel invisible, defeated and not good enough. So, while we are your biggest cheerleaders and secretly hope you never move out... don't forget to say thank you, take photos of us as proof we exist, and say "I love you." That is our fuel, our purpose, and what makes it all worth it.

Diapers to Driver's License

One day it hit me that my children would be adults. Part of me thought they would be babies forever. I always heard about the sleepless nights when you have a baby, and the endless diapers and piles of laundry. No one ever talked about raising teenagers and how much harder it would be. My generation was raised that we didn't earn a voice until we reached adulthood. I never wanted my children to not have a voice. I watched other parents hand over their phone or iPad to their kids and send them away. I would watch the meltdowns and the subtle shifts of behavior that gave a glimpse into their future.

I knew I was here as a mother to my children to be a teacher. Car rides were for lessons: We would talk about building credit at the age of 12, or blast music to shift the mood. We discussed issues and talked about what caused them and how to work through them. Each year that passed, we talked more and more and eventually we developed a safe relationship where we could talk about anything.

Don't bully your own children. You are their teacher. Your responsibility is to shape them into being a better person than you were. Help them learn how to grow and maintain their life well after you are gone. As adults, we think we are superior to those who are younger than us due to the lack of experience--but they are the future. Make the time to talk as often as you can.

TWELVE

Daddy's Girl

"One pill makes you larger and one pill makes you small,
And the ones that mother gives you, don't do anything at all.
Go ask Alice, when she's ten feet tall."
-White Rabbit by Jefferson Airplane

"They have each other, and we have each other. You are daddy's girl," he would say as he pet my hair and looked into my eyes with tears. I knew he loved me but deep down I felt alone. I didn't want to be his little girl. I wanted to be in my mom's and brother's club. I wanted my mom to tell me I was her mommy's girl. It wasn't fair that I was stuck with him. I didn't want his attention.

This man was a Jekyll and Hyde. When he loved, it was smothering and heavy. However, his happiness and charm were so abundant that the birds would sing. We had a beautiful childhood with that side of him. Pancakes for breakfast, road trips, Knott's Berry Farm and Disneyland were laced into days filled with sunshine and pool parties.

Through my childhood eyes, I remember Creedence Clearwater Revival would blast on the truck radio with the windows down. My hair would be twirling in the wind and hitting my face. The hot, dry air would fill my nostrils and the warm sun would settle onto my skin.

"I see a bad moon a-rising
I see trouble on the way
I see earthquakes and lightnin'
I see bad times today
Don't go around tonight
It's bound to take your life
There's a bad moon on the rise"

We pulled into a convenient store that was next to a little bar. He says, "I'll be right out," while his door squeaks open and his blonde hair and white shirt fade into a smokey bar. It's around noon and my brother and I were getting bored; it's been close to an hour. We scrape up loose change in the truck and head inside to the store.

I start picking through the individual candies. Ten cents for Bazooka bubble gum and five cents for jawbreakers. My brother dares me to steal one. I had never stolen in my life. I was only about seven or eight years old at the time, but my heart raced and I put a piece of gum in my jean pocket. I nervously laugh and shake in fear of being caught and taken away to jail. I then see a movie section and because we are bored kids that are killing time while our dad gets plastered next door, I wander in to browse through the movies. It was a small little room and it seemed kind of private. There was an older man in there browsing. I pick up a tape and start inspecting the title but I see the clerk running towards me and my brother is laughing hysterically. Is she going to arrest me for the gum? I look down at the tape, then all around me, and see naked people on these tapes. They're doing things I have never heard of or seen. I am horrified and the clerk comes in and grabs my arm and says, "Those movies aren't for kids, hun!"

We head back to the truck to wait. The sticky hot seats dampen with each minute that passes. My adrenaline is still rushing from taking the gum and from the embarrassment of walking into that room. We laugh until the bar door flies open and our dad is pushed out. He stumbles towards the truck, with blood on his shirt. Our smiles leave our souls and we straighten up our posture, putting our heads down to not make eye contact. The sun is setting and he falls into the truck, starts the engine and rolls out onto the roads, with the radio blasting. We watch as the front of the truck weaves back and forth, over the yellow lines, occasionally edging to the side of the road and then back to the other side. The stench of whiskey seeps out with every word he sings while struggling to keep his eyes on the road. We never know what is about to happen next, but the heaviness in my stomach burns while my legs shake as I am consumed with fear. Years later, when I became a teenager, he would tell me to never get in the car with someone who was drinking alcohol.

Eleventh Birthday

My dad comes home with his vibrant grin and a golden aura shining around him. His ocean blue eyes shimmered as he announced his victory of sobriety and flipped around his coin. We were always so proud of him each time he made it a substantial time without drinking alcohol. When he was sober, he was the best dad ever. His heart was bigger than anyone's and he was fun, adventurous, and charming.

I always knew when he would likely drink again. The happy mania would start wearing off and he would start cursing the sky, screaming at God with his middle finger up and his other hand balled in a fist. He would punch himself in the face, while his 6'4" stature blocked the doorway, as I watched the spit spew from his mouth in anger. Over time, I eventually saw him as an oversized child throwing a tantrum and felt sympathy for him rather than fear.

My mother would work full-time, including weekends and holidays, and she would come home and cook a homemade meal. I can't imagine how exhausted she must have been while chopping vegetables and preparing salmon after working all day, just to sit down, for the first time in hours, to enjoy a meal with her family. My dad would mutter something under his breath about the food being bland or tasting like shit. My mom was the best cook and still is. He would say it to hurt her. All I wanted to do was tell her how thankful I was and to tell him to stop, but I never knew how he would react.

My dad was a textbook case of bipolar disorder with a habit of self-medicating with alcohol. When he was sober he would go to church and when he was drinking he shunned religion. Every time he would pick up a drink again, my body would tense up. My breathing would become shallow and my legs trembled at the smell of alcohol on his breath, in fear of what would happen next.

I'd see him talking and laughing, then slyly pouring a drink as if it were never a problem. At first, he would be happy and joking around. As the day went on, he would start bumping into things. His smile slowly faded and his gleaming blue eyes turned into a dull grey. His soul would escape his body, leaving him with a hollow and desolate abyss that could morph into a demon at any moment.

DADDY'S GIRL

After this stage, anything could happen. Typically there would be a physical fight of some sort. Once, he picked my brother up by the neck and held him up against the wall as his feet dangled. Another time, while at a park, he fought several men. We left and he had blood all over his shirt. I watched this from the tire swing. Many nights he threatened to kill my mother. Every holiday it was a given that he would pour booze into a glass, and guard it closely as we waited for what was to come.

It was my eleventh birthday and it was still summertime. My mom took my friends and me to a local water park. I had about five friends sleeping over. It was still bright outside. It was 1996, so we were listening to cassette tapes: Toni Braxton, TLC, Spice Girls, and Ace of Base. We were just being girls in my room and then there was a loud sound. I stepped out of my room to see my dad standing over a pile of all my mother's clothes, ripping them apart with a large butcher knife.

My friends saw my smile fade. I tried to play it cool, but my voice became shaky and my nervousness filled the room with tension. I saw my brother run out and hide in the empty brick flowerbed. He couldn't be around when our dad drank or he became a punching bag. At this point, my friends were crying, holding each other in the corner behind the door. *These girls are never going to talk to me again,* I thought. A policeman came to my window and tried to calm us down. My mom had called the police and after my dad left, my friends called their parents to come pick them up. Those girls were never going to come over again and how could I blame them?

The 2nd to Last Father's Day

Father's Day is not always the easiest day for everyone. Some have lost their father and some have had an absent father. It can be an emotional day for many. Today is a day that I think about my dad, who has his phone turned off, so that his kids can't call and wish him a happy Father's Day. The last time we spoke was the previous week. I make sure to keep in contact daily but lately he forgets and sends hateful messages my way. When we spoke last week, everything was fine at first, but as he drowns his mind in his fifteenth can of beer, he turns into a broken man. His self-hatred consumes him to the point of misery.

My dad gave up on himself years ago. Each year that passes by, his mind and body transform more and more. Once a lean, handsome and charming man, he has turned into an overweight and grimy shell. He never made it to my wedding and now he can't even make it to the end of his driveway.

While taking Developmental Psychology as an elective for my associate degree, I fell in love with Erik Erikson's stages of psychological development. The theory identifies eight stages that healthy individuals should pass through. The stages vary from infancy to late adulthood. Each stage is characterized by a conflicting psychosocial crisis. In some stages, the individual can be stuck and will carry that virtue into the remaining stages.

In Erickson's stages, Generativity vs. Stagnation is when a person between the ages of 40-60 either volunteers, raises children, mentors or contributes to society. Generativity is finding your life's work and meaning. This stage is when the individual will either feel successful and fulfilled with their endeavors in productivity (family life, career, volunteering) or they will feel stagnant, unable or unwilling to help society, dissatisfaction, or self-centeredness. If you fail to accomplish this stage, you reach stagnation. Having little connection with others, lack of self-improvement and no motivation can be qualities of stagnation. Reflecting on your life at that age, you feel a sense of accomplishment or failure. My father, for example, lives in a state of despair. People in this stage feel as if their life is wasted. Erikson's theory helped me to realize why my father behaves the way he does. He is angry, bitter, self-medicating with alcohol, neglecting his health, and at times he can be emotionally abusive. This theory makes human behavior easier to navigate and understand, and perhaps teaches us a lesson to prevent going down a negative path as we age.

As the individual moves on to the last stage, Ego Integrity vs. Despair, which is late adulthood, they find themselves questioning their accomplishments, or lack thereof. If they feel their life has been successful, they will develop integrity. However, if the individual feels a sense of dissatisfaction and regret, they will develop despair and live the remainder of their life with depression and hopelessness. As my father transitions into this next stage, I realize he is clearly coming from stagnation. The next stage is Integrity vs. Despair, from the sixties till the end of life. Reflecting on your life at this age, you feel a sense of accomplishment or failure. My dad lives in a state of despair. People in this stage feel as if their life is wasted or they have unresolved regrets.

Though my dad has children and family who love him unconditionally, he takes his misery out on those he loves. I know when he calls me the worst names imaginable and repeatedly tells me that he hates me, that really he just hates himself. I know that he is a hurt man that feels hopeless with no answers. Maybe he carries regret for the years he was not sober. Years went by where I lived with a growing pit in my stomach of what the night would bring, as he swirled the ice cubes around in his empty glass. I believe he is a prisoner to his own mind and body.

Though he emotionally damaged my brother and me throughout our lives, we still remember our sober dad. We remember the road trips, Sunday breakfasts, camping trips and his great laugh. He has always been a Jekyll and Hyde. His soul felt the sunshine and other days he felt cold darkness. I blame everything on the ignored mental health crisis that no one talks about. I blame it on alcohol and how it can poison an unstable mind. I blame it on the world for looking the other way while others suffer, because they don't understand. As this elephant sits in the room, crushing others, we pretend to be fine.

My dad lies on his disintegrating bed, finishing a case of beer as his body gets sicker. His hate burns in his belly while he curses life. I don't know how long he will be around but I already grieve the idea of not having a father. I grieve that he won't let anyone help him and that we have to watch him slowly kill himself from afar, while his last words are that he hates us.

We just respond, "I love you too."

Sunday's Best

*Maple syrup on the dining room table adheres to my skin,
reminding me of Sunday's breakfast.*
*The sun was pouring through the window, illuminating the
dust in the air as it slowly floats.*
My dad was big and tall, like a lumberjack.
He flipped pancakes while singing along to Led Zeppelin.
*His smile was as warm as the butter melting on the plate he
made for us.*
This glimpse was like a family portrait on the wall.
It's Sunday's best, like what you see during a church service.
*Monday, Tuesday, Wednesday, Thursday, Friday, Saturday:
Those days were not the same.*
Those days were darker and they were not mundane.
*His smile faded as he wiped the liquor off his mustache,
swaying as his eyes showed someone else's soul.*
*Our bellies were not full from a happy family dinner, but a
deep aching pit of fear.*
*My legs would shake and my heart would race, wondering
how the night would end.*
Who would get hurt?
*I would hide in my closet, picking glitter and Barbie shoes
out of the corner as I heard screaming.*
Something would break.
*After the night became quiet and we all slept 'til morning, we
would wake up to Sunday's best version of him.*
*He remembered nothing as he kissed my forehead and went to
work.*
I always remembered everything he didn't.
*In the end, it was my turn to kiss his forehead, and for the
last time.*
His skin was cold and yellow.
*Just before he took his last breath, I told him I would
only remember Sunday's best.*

GARDEN OF BLU

It was Christmas, just before the SARS-CoV-2 pandemic became global news, known as COVID-19. My new Christmas tradition was family vacation: memories instead of gifts. Since my kids had two households, this meant two sets of holidays. They always made out well with gifts, so when I nervously asked if we could skip the stress of presents and trade it for travel, they agreed. We went to Austin, Texas and my mom came along. It was the first time we had been there, and I got to see my sister after so many years apart. We had amazing food, made unforgettable memories, and it was a great trip.

As much as I felt like I knew it was coming, I realize no one can truly be prepared. I got a text from my uncle, who lived with my dad, saying that my dad wasn't doing well. I had noticed my dad was talking less on the phone, saying he was tired often, and not responding to every text. I always called him every week and sent texts often but when he was harder to reach, I assumed he was just tired like he said. I immediately called my uncle and he told me that my dad was taken by ambulance to the ER. I knew that in the past when an ambulance was called for him, he would decline help. My uncle said he didn't know what year it was, which made it impossible for him to decline a trip to the ER.

I called the ER and was told that he was not in good shape and that my dad was very confused. My first thought was that his kidneys or heart were failing, until I was told that his skin was yellow. As soon as we unpacked, I had already booked a trip with my mom and brother to go to Missouri to see my dad. My cousin and his wife provided us a place to stay and a vehicle to use and we went to the hospital. Not knowing what to expect, we stopped at the doorway of his room and looked at each other, all taking a deep breath to brace ourselves. There he was, the man who brought me into this world and raised me. He was lying on his side, with long grey hair and a grizzly white beard. He was 63 but in just the previous year, he looked like he had aged 20 years. We had never seen him like this before.

We held his hands, kissed him, fed him ice cream, told him we loved him, and trimmed his beard. Our cousin, Jesse, brought his guitar to play music, giving my dad his own personal concert. After weeks of coming and going, dealing with insurance, making big decisions, and dreading what was to come, we realized it was time for the last goodbye. Here I spent so much of my life hating someone I loved. I had only just started repairing and mending the broken bonds of our relationship. I carried so much guilt for being too hard on him and not understanding that he was hurting.

There were times I would hold his hand and his eyes would open wide, he'd use the little strength he had to lift up his head to look into my eyes. I saw fear and I saw him wanting to say something. Instead the energy would drain from his body and he would drift back to sleep. I wanted to take away his fear. I wanted him to find peace and know how much we loved him. He couldn't let go. He was fighting for something and it was heartbreaking to watch. I asked the nurse why he was still holding on, why he couldn't just peacefully pass.

"Sometimes they just need to know you are going to be okay," she said.

I told my dad that we would all be okay. I told him how much we loved him and that it was okay for him to let go because we would only remember the good times. I ended with what he used to always say to us, "I love you more than love." On February 11th, 2020, my dad, Navy Seabee veteran Danny Guy Day Sr., passed away from cirrhosis of the liver.

I am grateful that I changed my perspective of him in time to be able to appreciate the time we had, despite watching him deteriorate. I am forever grateful for the staff on the 7th floor of Cox South Hospital for treating him so well. He loved his nurses and they went above and beyond. They even made sure he watched the Superbowl; his favorite team the Kansas City Chiefs beat the 49ers 31-20. He would tell us, "They sure are pretty," as the nurses fed him ice cream.

My dad loved to travel. He was a mountain man and photos from his past include him skinning snakes, catching fish, boating, road trips, BBQs and growing tomatoes. I used to want to be nothing like my dad because I only saw his flaws. Now more than ever, all I can see is the huge heart he had, his loving smile, funny nicknames, his laugh, his love for travel, and his good taste in music. I appreciate all of those qualities I gained from being his daughter. Now, when I find myself in nature or listening to Led Zeppelin, I think of him. I think of his contagious laugh and the sober dad who loved us all unconditionally. I think of all of our nicknames he gave us. I was Farty Pants and Miss Loo.

When you lose someone important in your life, all you can think about is what you miss. Just like his headstone reads, "In the end, love is really all that matters." I forgive my dad for being human. I love him despite everything. I would give anything to hold his hand again, and tell him I love him just one more time.

THIRTEEN

Booze Blues

"And what costume shall the poor girl wear to all tomorrow's parties
A hand-me-down dress from who knows where to all tomorrow's parties
And where will she go and what shall she do when midnight comes around
She'll turn once more to Sunday's clown"
-All Tomorrow's Parties by The Velvet Underground & Nico

When your friends come over with a bottle of wine and you laugh, distracting yourself from the stress in life, you pour another glass. The next day rolls around and there is still wine left, so you reward yourself after a long day by not wasting the remaining wine. The following day rolls around and you've worked a 14 hour day, with no time to eat, and finally sit down to order dinner at a restaurant. Next, you are sipping an ice cold beer while you wait for your meal. Suddenly, you are drinking more often than not. It becomes a habit. It's social, it's rewarding and it is intertwined into your daily routine.

We celebrate, we drink. We cry, we drink. The worst mixer for depression is alcohol. When you look into the mirror and hate what you see, you feel cursed, lost, and hopeless. For me, having a glass of wine seems to numb all of that emotional pain.

GARDEN OF BLU

Every morning after drinking, I would wake up feeling more depressed. Booze blues would take over my day along with a hangover. I didn't feel like talking, perhaps I was embarrassed if I drank too much, or from the careless choices I usually made. I felt like I was a broken mess of a person, and I was. I really was.

I never acknowledged that I had depression, at least not until my thirties. I never tried to heal myself mentally or to get stronger by loving myself because I simply did not care about myself. When you are there, at that moment, you don't see the reality of a downward spiral. You don't know that you are hurting yourself more or stalling your chance to grow and move forward. You're stuck, sometimes like quicksand, and you don't have the motivation to change. There seems to be no answer at that moment. Depression is like a desaturated and blurry lens over your view of life. I saw the world wrong and I needed glasses, but I didn't realize it because it was all I knew. I never saw the world any other way. I didn't slowly fall into a depression or suddenly get depressed after a big life-changing event. I was always living in the dark.

At night, drinking seemed to make me feel fun, extroverted, and confident. I didn't care about my hopeless problems. I had no self-worth. Working was the only thing that made me feel strong. When my children were away at their dad's house, I couldn't stand being alone in my quiet home. I was nobody on those nights. I was alone with my poisonous thoughts. Depression can eat away at you when you don't treat it or acknowledge it. It ate away at me. On my days with my children, I at least had a purpose. I made dinner, read stories and helped with homework. I was needed and loved. At times, however, I didn't even feel like I was even good enough for them.

BOOZE BLUES

In order to change, you have to choose to change. You have to wake the fuck up in order to see there is a choice in the first place. I remember the day when I looked in the mirror and decided it was time to get out of my current state of mind. I had just gotten out of the shower and stood in front of the mirror, looking at myself. I weighed the most I had ever weighed. I barely slept. I made terrible choices in relationships and had toxic friendships. I lived my life on the edge, constantly in fear of the unknown. My health was on the back burner. I was miserable. At that moment, I decided I was the only person that could make a difference in my life.

There is no one in the world that will rescue you besides yourself. Everyone has ups and downs in life and for some, the lows are really low. We all have damage but we must live in constant repair, just like a home needs repairs over time. However low you may be in a given moment is not an excuse to get lower or to stay there. It is an excuse to climb higher and to challenge yourself to be better, stronger, healthier, and happier. Life is all about training yourself to be a better version than yesterday, and you can't do that when you don't care about yourself.

Growing up watching Disney movies, I always dreamt of the fairytale. I dreamt that one day someone would swoop in on their horse and take me far away to some beautiful life. I would start over and have fields of flowers to lie in as my worryless mind focused on the blueness of the sky and the warmth of the sun. What I learned is that we are all knights in shining armour, but in our own lives, for ourselves.

The first step to healing is acknowledging what is broken in the first place, so that you can plan the route to repair. In this moment you can finally be awake, with a shifted perspective and a new awareness of yourself. We are always on the bottom of our own list of priorities and that needs to change. When they say, "you can't pour from an empty cup," it means that you cannot take care of your relationship, family, children, business, and other obligations when you are empty. Take care of yourself. It is an ongoing process and you will fall down. The difference is that you can get back up.

Now that I see people who hang out at the same bars that I once did, I wonder if they are struggling. On social media you see people smiling and having the time of their life, while beer bottles and cocktails decorate each photo. I see friends dying young, and no one sees it coming. They don't see it because they are living in a fog of blurry memories. They are buzzed and swaying to the latest song and laughing over last weekend's mistakes. They wake up hungover and start it over again.

What we don't see is that moment when they get home alone, if they go home alone. We don't see their struggles come back out as their buzz fades. We don't see what they battle or what they were trying to numb. We only see the fun side, the photos, the highlights, and the good times. Sometimes we don't see it until it's too late.

I wanted my memories to be clear and not blurry with hangovers and repeated mistakes. I knew that if I kept living this way, my memories would be in bars or with endless pouring wine on ladies night. I was ready to walk away and I had to. I was one of those young girls who didn't care what happened to her. I could have been someone who you'd never expect to lose, but I got out in time. I left the booze blues and went on to seek adventure through clearer lenses. I was crazy, wild, and a mess but my heart was frail and ready to fall apart.

I truly thought my friends would join me in this new idea I had: a life outside of alcohol. I didn't even care if they drank along the way, I just knew I wasn't going to. I made a post on Facebook, a call to action to summon new adventure buddies. I wanted to go kayaking, camping, traveling, to the botanical gardens, hiking, and to check out other cities nearby. In Florida, we have the luxury of taking short road trips to explore unique parts of the state. I had so many friends ready to be onboard. The reality was they didn't want to miss out on whatever party was happening. My circle of bar friends were just as miserable as I was. I also had several great friends that were there all along, but I was too busy giving my attention to the wrong ones.

It was time to make new friends during this process, which meant I would be hanging out alone more often. I didn't want to not see a new movie or not travel because I didn't have a friend or companion to join me. I refused to miss out on life because someone else needed to share the moment with me. I was often eating lunch alone, taking myself out to dinner, buying myself a gift for Valentine's Day, and truly getting to know myself and what I wanted out of life.

Removing alcohol from my life gave me the chance to understand who I was. I was able to focus on my career, become a better mother, start projects that I never had time for, find healthier hobbies, never have hangovers, lose weight, and find my self worth. I watched what alcohol did to my dad and I still allowed myself to fall down that rabbit hole. Becoming alcohol-free was the best decision I had made for myself. I had friendships forming with stronger bonds, less relationship issues, minimal drama, and I finally felt good about myself.

Many people are afraid to take that leap, because change can be ugly and uncomfortable. Growing is an ugly process and it can hurt and be very lonely and painful. It's so important to embrace alone time with yourself, though many fear it. This is when you really get to learn about who you are. Julia Roberts in *Runaway Bride* is a perfect example of how codependency and serial monogamist mentalities can hold us back from the much-needed relationship with ourselves. Julia Roberts' character is engaged for the fourth time and with each relationship, the way she prefers her eggs for breakfast changes based on her fiance's taste. She doesn't know her own identity, so she becomes a chameleon with each of her partners. Realizing she wasn't truly happy, she would run and leave her almost-husbands at the altar.

I can't help but wonder how many people do the same thing. I know I spent time in my life, in past relationships, liking the same style of eggs. It wasn't until I came out of a relationship that almost broke me, to realize who I was. I felt like such a failure with the end of yet another relationship. I had been chasing this person on and off since I was nineteen years old and this time it was over for good. I made the commitment to myself. I spent a solid six months being a broken shell of a woman. I like to null and void this block of my life, as I didn't know how else to cope. However, this low point is when everything shifted. The seedling was sprouting. It was exactly six months post-breakup when I looked into the mirror and decided to take control of my life and mental health.

Within two weeks, I landed a job I never thought I would get and was being flown to Chicago for training. The booze bloat melted off of my body and I felt good about myself. I spent the next six months dating me. Those six months of my life were monumentally impactful in shaping the woman I was becoming. If you haven't dated yourself yet, I highly recommend it.

Booze culture is highly glamorized and romanticized. Trending sayings like, "Rosé all day" and "Mommy's sippy cup," gloss over the toxic harm of normalizing routine alcohol consumption. I was part of that culture myself at one point, stating how I needed a glass of wine, or three, after a hectic day. Instead of finding balance, we drink. Instead of finding ways to practice self-care, we drink. Instead of seeing a therapist, we drink. We perpetually numb our emotions and never actually process or resolve them. It can and will creep up on you.

Do you find yourself drinking more days than not? What are you trying to numb? Whether you are trying to drown the reality of a major diagnosis, a loss, past trauma, or even just daily stress, it's time to find some healthy coping skills. For me, drinking was a distraction from facing my reality. It was a way to numb my mind and how I felt both mentally and physically. It was a way to break away from my quiet, unworthy self as alcohol loosened me up into a social butterfly. Whether it is a partner, friends, or family, you need to surround yourself with people who will support your goals, not enable your poor choices. You may have to purge and completely change your environment. You may even have to start over. Whatever distance you may need to go, it is worth it. I would go weeks and months at a time without drinking, but I always fell back into it because my friends and environment were the same. If I went out to a bar, I would order iced water in a rocks glass with lime, to look like I was drinking. It was much easier than having to explain why I didn't have a drink in my hand.

I was fortunate to not be addicted or unable to quit drinking. I wasn't an alcoholic to the point where I had withdrawals or needed to detox. I was able to just walk away and change my habits, friends, and environment. Drinking was more of a lifestyle and poor coping mechanism for me than an addiction. It is not that way for everyone. I encourage you to seek help if you need to. There is no shame in trying to heal and grow.

Once in a while I miss the idea of splurging on a fancy old fashioned or sharing a glass of wine on a holiday, but I remind myself of what comes with that choice. For me, alcohol is poison. It poisons my mind and my body feels it the next day. Instead, I fill my glass with sparkling water or make hot tea in a special tea set.

Celebrate everything in life, no matter how small. I have so much more fun since cutting booze out of my life. I have dinner parties where my friends come over and dress as goddesses in velvet with crowns as we eat charcuterie boards and pass around different strains of cannabis. We dress up to new themes, like 90s goth or PJs, while eating chocolate covered strawberries and working on art projects together. Find the excuse to dress up and have fun. Life is so short and we have the power to create new memories. Get a new hobby, go back to school, do the thing you secretly wish you could do. This is your fucking sign.

FOURTEEN

Grieving Your Past Self

"Yesterday is gone and you will be OK
Place your past into a book
Burn the pages, let 'em cook"
-Burn the Pages by Sia

Grieving is not something you only experience through the death of a loved one. It's something you feel when suffering through a loss. It's the distress of overwhelming pain and sorrow. Sometimes that loss is the life you dreamt of, or the life you once had. For some, their illness came suddenly, knocking them down during the peak of their career. For others, it's the loss of what could have been. It's the loss of what their body stole from them.

Someone healthy once said to me that people get sick because they want attention. That could not be further from the truth. You do not get attention when you are sick; you feel alone, unheard, and isolated. When a healthy person breaks their arm, they get condolences, cards, and cute little notes on their cast. For someone with chronic illness, it's nothing like that. Instead, it's redundant and a broken record. People don't often understand the reality of chronic illness. Many times, we don't even speak about our illness, or at least we try to limit it when we do. We are told that we are too negative, too lazy, or that it's all too much to handle. When someone asks how our day is, we often try to make them more comfortable by saving them from the awkwardness of responding with the truth. "I'm fine," we'll say.

When I was single, I usually forewarned whoever I was dating that I had heart issues. I always figured it was the right thing to do. What if it was too much for them? Usually, it was not an issue. Many times I would even go to the Emergency Room and not even tell them. I didn't want anyone to worry about something that was normal for me. Of course, later down the road, in some relationships, my chronic illness felt like a burden. There was this one person I was dating; it was light, fun, and casual, and then things started to get serious. Though I am not sure if what comes next was fueled by uncertainty; at the time I wasn't ready for a relationship and was sometimes distant and cold. I got dumped. I didn't get dumped because I was aloof and uncertain as to what I wanted, but it was because of my heart. I was told, "I don't know if I want to get involved with someone who has heart issues. Like, what if you died? Or, what if I had to take care of you all the time? It's just... too much. Sorry."

In another relationship, I was told that I was a hypochondriac. I have been told that I always complained about something, or that they "can't keep up" with all of my ailments. With friends, I have been called a flake. Don't get me wrong, I earned that title during one phase of my life, but most of the time I was bailing on plans due to my health. Though close friends understood, new friends or acquaintances did not. With chronic illness, your invitations to outings and events tend to be less and less frequent. I felt forgotten and realized many of my "friends" were only drinking buddies or a wingman. Out of sight, out of mind. People moved on from my presence and gravitated towards a replacement.

With work, I would fake being healthy in the beginning. Eventually I would lose my job due to absences, even after later explaining my health. I would get a new job, and the cycle continued. Some jobs, like bartending, were easy to get away with because the hospitality industry can be flexible. Most people are in school, single moms, or have a second job to juggle. I didn't want to be a bartender forever. Then, I finally had a dream career that was flourishing. I was traveling several times per year, all expenses paid for. I was challenged, inspired, thriving, and growing. But, my health always catches up; it always knocks me down, no matter how high I climb. I was constantly starting over or digging myself out of the hole after each flare, only to crash and burn again. Typically, I would quietly climb back up. I kept most of my health to myself, besides major things that were hard to hide. I masked my symptoms. Depression was always tucked away inside. I never slept and I resented my body. Finally, I didn't climb back up. I accepted it. I embraced it. I shared my story and my truth so that others didn't feel the need to suffer silently like I did. My career fell apart and someone replaced me.

On the plus side, when my health had deteriorated, I realized who was important. I realized I wasted precious time with the wrong people when I had amazing friends that were there all along. It reminded me about quality over quantity. I have learned to change my perspective. I may not be the career-fueled woman I once was, but my passion has never skipped a beat. I remind myself how grateful I am to now live a more genuine life. My life is a challenge, but it is real and so are my relationships.

When you find yourself in this position, it's a chance to reinvent yourself. You get to reevaluate everything. You can cut the toxins out and you ask yourself, what do you truly want? Sometimes those toxins are people. I may be grieving who I once was, my fair-weather friends, and my fast-paced career; however, I am excited to see how my new journey unfolds and where life will take me. I felt that my purpose needed to be more meaningful. I was lost in the fun, excitement, and the haze of fake friends and I couldn't see what I was meant to do. I used to feel like it was me against the world. I felt so alone, and now I realize that there are so many of us. We have our own community, where technology has made our connections possible. I remember the days when social media didn't exist. There were no support groups. No one taught me how to advocate for my health. Today, together we all share our voice and make grieving life with chronic illness a little less painful.

Elisabeth Kübler-Ross was a Swiss-American psychiatrist who came up with the five stages of grief model: denial, anger, bargaining, depression, and acceptance. These stages are not linear and not everyone fits this model. For chronic illness, we have many sub-stages, and the framework is more of a mess. For some, the stages just cycle over and over or we get stuck in one stage. For many, we balance life in the acceptance stage and then suddenly find ourselves feeling angry. Identifying these feelings can help you to feel less alone while making sense of your emotions.

Shock and Denial

I can't count how many times I have sat in my doctor's office, begging for new tests or blood work. I often hope that somehow we missed something and that all I need to do is a minor change and then I can be healthy. Then, my blood work comes back and everything is "normal." How can I possibly feel this way forever?

Denial is finally getting the answers you have been searching for and then wanting to light those answers on fire and get a redo. Denial is working full-time when your body isn't cut out for it, but you have bills to pay and mouths to feed. Instead, you work all day until you come home and collapse in bed, too exhausted to shower, as every cell in your body is in agonizing pain. Denial is smiling through a conversation with a friend as your vision fades, your limbs go numb, and there's ringing in your ears. You know this wave of presyncope will pass as you hold onto the wall. You don't want to say anything because it's normal for you and you want to be normal for them. "I'm just tired," you say.

Blame and Guilt

You may find yourself doing something mundane, like brushing your teeth, and then suddenly you burst into tears. You comb through the past, wondering if there was something you did wrong or if you just took better care of yourself, that things would be different.

"Why me?"

Maybe you did everything by the book: you ate your vegetables, you were always positive, and you even tried yoga. But, here you are: suffering. It isn't fair. What makes it worse is that people give their unsolicited advice, suggesting exercise. When you do exercise, your heart rate skyrockets, you feel dizzy, you spend the next 24 hours in bed, or bronchial spasms and chest pain take over. Of course we all love the, "heal your childhood trauma," as you are already in therapy and read all the latest self-help books.

"Maybe if you changed your diet or tried this supplement..."

Though, you are likely already on a strict diet due to food sensitivities and already incorporated vitamins into your medicine routine. What haven't we tried? Some of these suggestions may help, but it doesn't put a dent into our mountain of health issues. These suggestions plant a seed in your brain, making you question if you caused this. Remember that you did not cause this.

Anger

There are moments when I am pissed off and furious. I am exhausted and in pain and so very angry. In these moments I feel so utterly disheartened and hopeless; however, these moments pass. It is important to not live here, in this stage of grief. Continuing to fight and stay positive is a challenge on its own, and anger is healthy in small doses. It's okay to not be okay, and it's okay to feel the lows. Find an outlet, hobby, support group, therapist, or start journaling. Using anger as fuel for motivation is something I have always strived for. "Tomorrow is a new day," I would grunt to myself while rolling my eyes. I allowed myself to be angry that day, eating ice cream, and letting my body recover. Tomorrow will be a new day. We will try again then.

Bargaining

Bargaining is when you tell yourself that this new diet is going to make you feel better. You convince yourself that if you become more spiritual, more physically active, or more positive that maybe your outcome will change. Yes, lifestyle changes have a profound impact. I always say that you have to give your body a fighting chance with nourishment, hydration, stress management, a healthy diet, quality sleep, and self-care. Do not confuse this with not taking responsibility, as sometimes we can only do so much and STILL find ourselves sick. Know that the grieving process with chronic illness is a rollercoaster. We often think that maybe we aren't trying hard enough, and part of the bargaining stage is desperately trying hard to find a solution.

Depression and/or Anxiety

You can hide it and you can pretend it doesn't exist, but depression and anxiety are very much an aspect of chronic illness. Depression is the feeling of impending doom, but that feeling sticks around even if you are happy or having a good day. It slithers into your existence and it isn't always tied to a memory or life experience. Anxiety is the nervous butterflies in the pit of your stomach that grow into your chest. Positively thinking it away is not a thing, and depression is not always something you can control.

Though depression and anxiety do not discriminate, they can be more prevalent in the disabled or chronically ill community. Imagine building up your goals and life-long dreams. Your ambitious personality and positive mental attitude kicks ass and you have the world at your fingertips, but you keep getting knocked down due to uncontrollable circumstances: your health. Sure, you can dust yourself off and try, try, try again. The reality is, it's hard and it sure gets old when decades go by and you watch your peers buy houses, new cars, start a family, and live successful lives. Meanwhile, you try to figure out how you can afford not having income for weeks or months at a time as you recover from surgery, balancing which medications you can afford while making sure there is enough money left over for a cheap dinner. You then start over, just to ride the big wave until you crash again.

It can also be lonely, even when you have supportive friends and family. It's a place that not many people understand. Chronic illness is an unpaid full-time job. It's exhausting and scary. Support groups are very helpful; finding a community of people with similar health issues helps you cope, not feel alone, and also educates you on your illness. Anxiety is an issue as well because having a chronic illness can be traumatic. For example, I have Wolff-Parkinson-White Syndrome and my heart rate would get up to the 250s daily. I have also had many scary arrhythmias, so when I hear the hospital heart rate beeping sound on a TV, it gives me major anxiety. It is a trigger for me, as well as fast rhythmic tapping. It is always nerve-wracking to wonder when the next episode or flare will hit.

It is absolutely crucial that you manage your mental health. Do not be afraid to ask for help. Check your local resources if you are uninsured. Join support groups, see a therapist, and make it a priority. Mental health is just as important as your physical health. I repeat: Mental health is just as important as your physical health.

Acceptance

Put your warrior paint on! You have your medical records organized, and recent tests and labs done. You are making progress with answers or even starting new treatments. You got this! Or maybe you don't, but you have just accepted the cards you are handed and will make it work. This stage varies for many and is a sliding scale. For some, it could mean you are managing. For others, this stage comes and goes, varying based on what condition your health is in. Again, this process is not linear… It's a scribble!

You might visit the land of acceptance often. Maybe you have a beach house here, or maybe you're planning a vacation here, but you likely won't retire here. We are nomads of this grieving process. We jump around, visit, flip flop between two stages and circle around.

Acceptance is the best place to be. It's when we feel really positive, and not just faking it. It is when we fight for awareness and advocacy. It is when we make progress or actually have a less painful day. It's when your treatment is manageable and you're coasting. Find a purpose, like sharing your story, becoming an advocate, or raising awareness of your condition. This helps to coast in the acceptance stage a little longer, being fueled by helping others to not feel alone.

Purpose

We don't always fully accept our loss, and that's okay. Sometimes I feel like I drive myself crazy trying to find acceptance. What has helped me, is finding my reason or purpose for the pain and suffering I have endured. Raising awareness helps others to feel less alone, while also helping others discover a diagnosis.

Awareness also paves an easier path for those who are following a similar journey. Awareness is activism. What will the purpose from this pain or loss inspire?

FIFTEEN

Pardon the Mess While I Grow

Tyler Durden: "It's only after we've lost everything that we're free to do anything." -Fight Club

I was extremely shy my entire life, and after cosmetology school and bartending, my shyness was long gone. I was in a new season of life, where the shy version of myself had been tucked away. I became a social butterfly. I was building my empire, helping the community, networking, and I knew everyone. I truly thought I had so many friends. It was not until my health was at a low point when I realized that I actually only had a handful of real friends: those who visited when I had open heart surgery, those who came by when I got my pacemaker, those who checked in on me when my dad passed away, and those who were there during other difficult times.

When I shared the reality of my health, I felt dropped and as if I had become a has-been. I felt forgotten and realized most of my friends were only drinking buddies or they just preferred the fun side of me. Out of sight, out of mind. People move on from you and gravitate toward a replacement. My health always catches up like a tornado. I kept most of my health issues to myself besides major surgeries that were hard to hide. I masked my symptoms with caffeine, marijuana and alcohol. I never slept and I resented my body.

I eventually shared my struggles so that others didn't feel the need to suffer silently like I did. My hair clients slowly started to fade away. I would scroll through social media and find a client checked in at a different salon. Even friends would try to justify not calling me by saying, "I know you don't feel well," or "I figured you needed space." They made that decision for me, even though I never felt well my entire life and I previously hid it. Everything changed once I became transparent. Remember, the shell of a person has no correlation to what is inside. You never know what battles lie within others.

I was always seeking fun and distractions with people who were equally broken, when I had loving friends standing by. I was ready to enter a new chapter in life, with no toxic friendships, no false relationships, and nobody with a hidden agenda sucking the life out of me. I created my own career that caters to my needs and allows me to juggle my weekly medical appointments. I became my own boss.

How can I touch lives and make a difference? What is my purpose? What makes me happy? How can I live my best life with these circumstances? Toxins are not just in food or beauty products, but it can be people, relationships, your job, or your current state of mind. As a coping mechanism, instead of trying to heal and help myself, I helped everyone else.

Anxiety is not being nervous over a big presentation at work. It's not the butterflies in your stomach while you stress over what to wear. It's not the feeling of having a hard time because you have too much on your plate. Anxiety is a wave that towers over you, consuming your entire body. You tremble and shiver, your throat closes up and your palms sweat. Your heart races like a hummingbird. Many times it can be for no reason at all. It is out of your control. Your body is temporarily not yours. A state of panic sets in and you feel like you might die. Anxiety is neurotransmitters out of balance.

Depression is not feeling bummed because you had a rough day. It's not feeling sad because things didn't go your way today. It is not something that you can just suck up and get over. It is not cured by a simple attitude adjustment. It is a thick heavy blanket that drowns you. Sometimes it is devastatingly painful. Sometimes it is pure numbness, and other times it is the feeling of doom buried deep within you. It is like you are grieving the biggest loss you have ever felt. Even when the sun is shining and the sky is blue, this feeling can sink you. Oftentimes there is not even a reason. It's like you're missing a limb. Something is missing but you can't place what it is.

Anxiety and depression don't make you weak, nor does it mean you are weak. Mental health disorders are greatly misunderstood by a majority of society. The stigma must end and something needs to change. Generations are losing many to this epidemic. Addiction grows from mental health disorders and the need to self-medicate to escape from suffering.

Acknowledging the status of my mental health was a huge step towards healing myself. Because I had removed alcohol from my life, I stopped distracting myself from my problems and started to sort through them. Instead of letting a feeling or emotion consume me, I asked myself why I was feeling that way.

Another huge factor was working on my bitterness. I was so angry at the world. I felt so wronged and unlucky. When I worked on lightening up and becoming more patient, I also learned to be more forgiving. I went from, "fuck my life," to "okay, I can get through this."

How to Work Through a Problem

Life can be unpredictable, chaotic, stressful, out of balance and just straight up crazy. It is vital to our mental health to be able to manage the stress in our lives in a healthy manner. Unfortunately, we are not born with the knowledge of balancing mental health and the inevitable stressors that life throws our way. We surely did not learn this in home economics class either. We are thrown to the wolves and some of us figure it out, while others are hiding in their bathroom with chocolate and tears.

People naturally gravitate towards a way of relief from the lemonade raining in our lives. For some, that relief is alcohol, drugs, shopping, gym, sex, and so on. Addictions come in many forms and with many masks. You may not even realize that you have your own demons because it is packaged neatly in a decorative glass that says "Mommy's Happy Juice." Your addictions may be something with healthy attributes, like going to the gym. Only, you work out more than you do anything else and you have developed an obsession with your workout routine, schedule, nutrition and progress. Or, maybe you don't self-medicate, but you isolate yourself from your friends, you stop doing the things you enjoyed once, and maybe you've started having anxiety attacks.

In a nutshell, stress makes us do weird things. It makes us sick, or sicker. It steals the joy out of life when it is not under control. It tears relationships apart. It throws hurdles in our way and derails our plans. It imprisons us in a haze of distractions while our problems pile up. It stunts our ability to grow and elevate.

In my Introduction to Healthcare class, our first assignment involved the problem-solving process using the Scientific Method. I am sharing what I learned so that you can apply this five-step process to areas in your life that may benefit from finding a solution.

Problem:

What is your problem? Maybe it is something huge and overwhelming or it could be something small and petty that could get swept under the rug. Regardless of the size, every issue should be dealt with because they add up and they grow. They fill up your cup and overflow. The next thing you know, you are drowning.

Tip: Keep a small notebook. Create lists of goals, tasks, issues, solutions, progress, failures, etc.

Fact: It is okay to fail. Think of it like you just took one for the team and learned something from it; now you can share your failure and knowledge with others so that they can grow from it like you did. Failure is awesome. It builds character and wisdom. It's a challenge and it comes with lessons and stories. It is far from boring and it fuels fire and births bravery… if you allow it. Perspective is everything. Many successful people would not be where they are today without the failures that happened throughout their journey. Even if you fail, you never really lose.

You learn and you have the opportunity to see what is next. Sometimes it is the universe taking you towards a different path. It is a beautiful part of life, depending on what you make of it.

Step One - Identify the Problem

Observe the full picture. What is the root of the issue? What is the cause? Are there other factors involved? Look beyond the obvious.

Example: I hate my job and it makes me miserable.

Step Two - Gather Information

Decisions influenced by opinions and emotions may result in poor outcomes. What are the possible solutions and outcomes? What are the facts? What do you feel? What do you want? What or who would be a reliable source of information in reviewing options? What could be the consequences or risks? Ask yourself some questions. Write it down if you need to.

Example: Why do I hate my job? Is it the environment, coworkers, boss, career field or the hours? What is causing me to be unhappy at my place of work?

Step Three - Create Alternatives

We are finding solutions to our problems, not problems with our solutions. Create a list of options, both positive and negative.

Example: Ask for a raise. Go back to college. Update your resume and actively search your job field for opportunities. Find out if you can move to a different position; perhaps you don't feel challenged or fulfilled in your current position. Do some soul-searching: are you depressed and your job is affected by your mood instead of the other way around? Try changing up your environment by promoting weekly group challenges to boost morale, or doing squats before lunch while answering phone calls, or getting to know coworkers better by planning a night out.

Step Four - Choose an Alternative and Take Action

This is an important step. What is the point of steps 1-3 if we aren't going to actually get our hands dirty and make a real effort to resolve this issue? If some of your alternatives are extreme or risky, try the other options first if you want to be on the side of caution. Multi-tasking solutions is also a possibility since some alternatives may take more time than others. Some alternatives may be a quick fix while you work on another alternative that may be more of a long-term solution.

Example: "I really want to go back to college and change careers but it would be a huge process, expensive, a lot of work and a big challenge. I am going to try to make friends with my coworkers and build those relationships and then ask my boss for new responsibilities and a raise." This is a great start, but keep in mind those were problems for the first solution. Going back to college may be a big challenge but it could be worth it and it could be the best solution. Don't create problems to scare off a possible solution. However, working with the other alternatives first is a great idea while you investigate the other options.

Step Five - Evaluate and Revise as Needed

Now it is time to review your results. What has been effective or ineffective? At this point, you can adjust your alternatives or fine-tune them. Revise your plan until you sort out the best solution.

Example: You decided you are just not passionate about your job and your boss can't afford to promote you. You decide to go back to school but this will be a process, so you enroll in online classes. To make the long-term process more enjoyable, you build relationships with your coworkers and convince your boss to allow casual Friday pizza day to boost morale. You also started listening to podcasts while you work and got a cat to help improve your mood when you go home.

Hopefully this outline has helped or inspired you to work through stressful situations or problematic times in your life. If you still find that you can't manage stress, look into getting professional help like seeing a therapist. There may also be local resources in your area to help get through certain issues.

SIXTEEN

Self-Care

"In every life we have some trouble
But when you worry you make it double
Don't worry, be happy"
-Don't Worry Be Happy by Bobby McFerrin

Cutting out a toxic work environment or toxic relationships can be difficult, but we tend to forget that sometimes we are being toxic to ourselves. We judge ourselves, punish ourselves, and shame ourselves, sometimes on a daily basis. In fact, we judge ourselves harder than anyone else. We get in our own way. It is time to get yourself off the back burner and turn up the heat. You deserve the love you give to everyone else.

I grew up in a generation where it was considered selfish to put yourself first or to do anything for yourself. Especially as a woman, my generation was raised carrying baby dolls while our mothers placed a hot, home cooked meal on the table at 6:00 p.m. We give, give, give until there is nothing left of us. It can be difficult to survive in a one-income family, leaving both people in the relationship working. At the end of the day, we still get stuck in those same traditional roles, yet with completely different variables. I am always a huge fan of breaking stigmas and stepping out of traditional roles.

Yoga

I always try to be active in some way, even if it is minimal. It can be very difficult when I lack the motivation or energy, but losing muscle tone or having my muscles atrophy is a big fear of mine with having a chronic illness. It is especially an issue with Ehlers-Danlos Syndrome because of a collagen defect, which causes subluxation and wonky unstable joints. Losing muscle can increase instability and create even more problems as well as cause deconditioning. Yoga has been a struggle for me due to low blood pressure, dizziness, and instability in my wrists, which make it painful to do some poses. However, I absolutely love breathing exercises and finding moments of peace. I can't recall how many times I have forgotten to breathe. It's like the instructor is in my head. "Don't forget to breathe," she says as I finally exhale and release the tension in my body. It helps me to focus on my body and the awareness of what is stiff, painful, weak, needs strength, and the amount of tension I hold in my body. Yoga also helps reduce my back pain.

The pros outweigh the cons. Truthfully, I have enough excuses to not ever do yoga. I hear many reasons from others with similar health issues that swear it is horrible for them. Perhaps it is but many forget that we can tailor anything to our needs. I choose to modify yoga to MY needs. My wrists won't handle the downward dog pose. Does that mean I give up? Absolutely not. Instead, I do downward dog for the three seconds I can handle, giving my wrists a chance to build strength without hurting myself, and then I convert into Table Top position. I will also never do the camel pose again, after the last time it put me into a severe vertigo episode.

Here is where most people go wrong: they are so afraid of what others will think. People are afraid to be different and they are afraid of judgment. I dare someone to ask me why I am the only one in a different pose. Judge me. Frankly, I don't give a shit. I am here for me, not them. There was an instance where I attended a morning beach yoga session and being in Florida during July, it gets brutally hot. Halfway through the class, the sweat was dripping down my nose. Salty sweat burned my eyes and at one point, the breeze was gone. I was overheating, miserable and dizzy. My solution was to get up mid-pose and walk to the water. The water was so cool and refreshing. I was so happy to dive in and rinse the cool water over my arms, washing away the sand. I felt like a kid again. I didn't feel like a failure for giving up or not making it through class. I was doing what worked for me and my body. When I came back to my towel, I sat in a basic pose that may or may not have been yoga, and I closed my eyes and focused on my breathing and the sound of the ocean. I did this until class ended.

After class was over, everyone ran into the water to cool off. We all headed back and one woman came up to me and said that she admired me for getting into the water. She said, "I was fantasizing and almost hallucinated about getting in the water too. It was hot!" Everyone complained about how miserable the heat was and I could not help but wonder why they sat there melting away. They were not focusing on breathing or their body but daydreaming about the time moving faster so that the class could end. They suffered through, unhappy and distracted because they didn't want to be different or to be judged. Why do we invent non-existent expectations from others? Strangers even! I am so glad I made it to yoga that day, even though I did things my way. I don't look at it as giving up. I showed up. I tried my best. I did what worked for me. Instead of not trying at all, create your own version. You know your body and your limits. Each time you train or practice for anything, it will always be your best version. You can't top it without showing up again. You do not have to be perfect and you need to stop comparing yourself to everyone else.

Climbing the Goal Mountain

Setting goals can be exciting, yet intimidating. How many times have you set a goal that felt out of reach, so you just let it collect dust? I was tired of having so many goals while I never made any progress towards them. I dream big, so these dreams felt completely out of reach. I decided I needed to look at things differently. When setting long-term goals, typically you need to cross off smaller goals to get there. When I decided that I wanted to go back to school, I found out I owed $550 and needed to retake a couple of classes that I half-assed ten years ago.

My first thought was… forget it. After deciding that I didn't want to give up, I slowly saved up to pay off my previous student balance. I reapplied to the college I went to and paid the admissions fee. I retook two classes, which in total took me over a year to cross everything off my list. Ultimately, I got in the groove of being a student and eventually became a college graduate. Looking back, I realize how easily it could have been to not waste my time, to save my money, and to find a new plan.

My goal was not easy, in fact, it was a long struggle. When you break down your big, long-term goal into a list of smaller goals, it becomes more achievable. You cannot get to the top of a mountain without taking several steps. Map out your journey and come up with a game plan for each step to get there.

Burnout

Self-care is all about learning how to say no, balancing all aspects of your life, and finding that good flow in life. I used to equate success with being busy. I would work 14 hour days and often go without a day off. I felt like I was on top of the world, thriving with my career. Realistically, I was burning the candle at both ends and then dousing the candle in gasoline. I was burnt out. I lived many years with burnout and didn't even realize it. Burnout is the state of mental, emotional, and physical fatigue caused by stress, overworking, and the imbalance of juggling everything in your life.

When someone is experiencing burnout, self-care is on the back burner. There is just no time. I would be so exhausted that spending the time to cook a fresh meal was not happening. Going to the grocery store might be too much effort. Whatever is left in the fridge needs to be tossed. Suddenly, ordering pizza or takeout is looking really good. Though sometimes ordering food can be an act of self-care, it can turn into a routine of self-sabotage and bad habits really fast.

I always know when I am headed to or in a state of burnout when I order takeout more than once a week. Not only am I paying more for delivery fees for mediocre food that is barely warm, but I am not nourishing my body. I am not in balance and I am crumbling as I neglect myself. After your diet and nutrition goes out the window, fatigue is next. We become deficient in vitamins and our brain and body does not have enough time to recover and decompress. Brain fog and a shitty mood follow. Congratulations, you've officially crashed and burned.

As much as I know and understand how to prevent burn out, sometimes I still slide backwards and have to be reminded that I am headed to that state. It made me wonder what about my personality made me flock to a stressful schedule and to flood my calendar. I then asked myself, what do I feel like when I am not so busy? Of course, I revel in the moments of peace and being in nature but I think it's because I know it is temporary. I will be right back to the chaos. I know my dream would be to live in that moment, in peace, surrounded by beauty. But in that daydream, there are no stipulations and no responsibility. The dream is to simply exist and live a simple life, right? The reality is that life is not so simple. We have bank accounts, health issues, children who need raising, and bills to pay. I would always need to live near hospitals, pharmacies, and medical facilities.

Since I can't live in that dream, I do in fact have to worry about paying my bills and scheduling doctors appointments. I find myself falling into the downward spiral of staying busy. Then it hit me. I was distracting myself from the chronic pain, past traumas, and suffering I endure. I stay busy to avoid emotional distress. It is a way to cope with my baggage, to bury it deep under each plan and activity I place in front of me. When I realized what I was doing was not completely healthy, I initially felt disappointed in myself. Then I realized that this is how I respond to the trauma in my life and my state of health. I live with a progressive and incurable disorder that might take my life one day. I then took away the harsh judgement I gave myself as I know I could handle it worse. I once handled it much worse and I know this means that I will one day handle it even better than I do now.

Another act of self-care is to look back, to the present, and ahead. When we reflect, we can often see how much we have grown. When we look into this very moment, we can compare from the past while also planning how much we anticipate to grow from here. In the grand scheme of things, we can comprehend the whole picture and realize that we are moving forward, even if it seems slow. Then, take a deep breath and remind yourself that you are doing a good job. You don't need to hear it from anyone but yourself. So, say it.

Devoting Time For You - Therapy Thursdays

Self-care is not selfish. It is also not simply taking your vitamins and going to see your doctor--that is health management. Self-care is devoting time to focus on yourself. I spent one entire semester going on adventure, traveling around Florida to places that were on my bucket list, going to the springs or having an acai smoothie bowl on the beach. I did this every Thursday and called it my Therapy Thursday. Sometimes I spend these days alone, walking nature trails with sunglasses on as I cry and listen to music or podcasts. Other times I would have friends join me and we would laugh until our cheeks hurt.

Taking the time to decompress each week was incredibly therapeutic, but also it was the most balanced I had felt in a long time. We need one day to recover from the week and another day to decompress and have fun. The most common excuse I hear when I try to explain Therapy Thursday to others is, "I don't have the time," or "I wish I could have time for that." I call bullshit. You can make the time for anything that you make a priority. It took me at least a full year to truly respect my Therapy Thursday mission. I marked my calendar to say, "NO FUCKING WORK!"

for every Thursday, yet still booked meetings, clients, and work. I didn't listen to myself. If you can't take a day, take a morning. Figure it out. It took me almost a year to finally make this my new habit. It's your life after all. When you sacrifice too much of yourself, you will be left with nothing else to give. Self-care is the foundation of giving and nurturing others.

Once I got into the routine, people started to know that on Thursdays I would be unavailable. Doing this has allowed me to be more patient. I was managing my stress levels well and didn't take out my frustrations and exhausted mental health on others by snapping at people I cared about. Instead, I could give others the best version of me. I could breathe. I soon realized how important it was for my mental health when the following semester I overbooked myself and squeezed out my Thursdays. I got burnt out fast. I was miserable, impatient, and moody. Lesson learned.

Self-care does not always have to involve going on adventures, spending money, or bougie treats. Self-care can be establishing a morning ritual, like spending 30 minutes each morning outside with a cup of tea, reflecting on gratitude and growth. Self-care can be listening to music while walking in nature. It can be journaling, long bubble baths, or just spending the day in bed with Netflix and ice cream. Whatever it may be, it should bring you a little bit of peace. Always find ways to sprinkle joy into your life.

No.

Self-care can also be saying no. Do you ever feel the need to have an excuse ready or to explain your reasoning behind saying no? I noticed that I always felt obligated to explain myself, even if it meant coming up with an excuse instead of saying that I am tired. Here is a tip for you: you don't have to explain shit.

How to say no without bullshit excuses:

- I can't. Maybe another time!
- Raincheck!
- Sounds fun, but I am going to pass this time.
- No, I can't tonight, but thank you for the invite.

And if someone says no to you, accept it. Mind your own business.

Remember to breathe. Take a deep breath. Take another deep breath and relax your shoulders. Unclench your jaw. Take a deep breath through your nose and exhale through your mouth, feeling each breath.

How To Glow Up

- Surround yourself with people who are proud of you, not jealous of your accomplishments.
- Share your story. One day your struggles will light the path for someone else.
- The only diet you need is replacing toxic people with tacos.
- It is okay to reinvent yourself if life throws you off the path you chose.
- Self-care is not a luxury, it is the foundation of health and

wellness. Make it a priority.

- Acknowledge your mistakes or you will hinder your growth.
- The person you need to forgive the most is yourself. Forgive the past versions of yourself. Those are the lessons that you grew through.
- Self-love is the key to balance and wellness, and a must for any relationship.
- Set boundaries and stick to them.
- Your worth is not based on your caloric intake or how many times you hit the gym this week.
- Never stop advocating for yourself, because by doing so you are advocating for others.
- If you are chronically ill, you are still worthy as fuck.
- Stay hydrated.
- Let go of the bullshit. If you don't, it will give you wrinkles.
- Pay it forward and help others.
- Doubt is the disease of passion. It is nothing but a weight that drags you down. Get out of your own way.
- Instead of focusing on what you will lose, focus on what you will gain. Sometimes things must fall apart in order to fall into place. In the waves of change you will find a new direction.
- Success is not defined by how busy you are. You are only too busy to make time for people or things that are not a priority and it shows.
- You are never the asshole if you remain cool, calm, and collected.
- Apologize for hurting someone you care about, even if you don't understand or agree.

- Forgive, even if you didn't get an apology. It is for you, not them. And by forgiving, that doesn't mean they need to know or come back into your life.
- Remember that when you are a tornado, your winds affect those around you. The energy you emit is felt by others.
- Your self-limiting thoughts hold your future hostage. If you think you can't then you won't. Fear is a prison you have the key to.
- You can respectfully listen without obeying an opinion. Opinions are not orders.
- Make some day be today.

SEVENTEEN

How to Listen to Your Body

"All the pain and the truth - I wear like a battle wound
So ashamed, so confused - I was broken and bruised
Now I'm a warrior"
-Warrior by Demi Lovato

I t is so important to learn how to tune into your body. Sometimes we all just get carried away with life and run through the motions. We procrastinate and the next thing you know, days turn into weeks and suddenly weeks become years. We never know our own baseline because we can't comprehend the changes second by second. Only others can see the changes in us, as they see lapses in time and how we morphed since the last time they saw us.

I challenge you to be mindful of what your norm is and what your body's baseline is. Don't be a stranger to your own body. Don't you have folders in your office for important things like school, taxes, or work? What about your health? Think about planning a wedding. It is one special day and we spend a year or two with a planner, folders, Pinterest boards, and magazines—but when it comes to our own health, we don't even make half that effort. Why is that? It's time to change this mentality.

A few common signs can be visible ways your body communicates with you. These signs are your intelligent body's way of saying, "Hey! Look at me!" It's waving a red flag.

1. **Dry Skin**: Is your skin dryer than usual? Are your lips chapped? These may be signs that you are not staying as hydrated as you need to be. Other signs to look for include constipation and dark urine. Not staying well hydrated could also include symptoms of fatigue and dizziness. Of course many symptoms can overlap with other issues but on a general level, checking your skin can give you an idea that your body needs something. Sjogren's Syndrome can also cause dryness in the mouth, throat, eyes, and skin. Hypothyroidism, psoriasis, dermatitis, eczema, and diabetes have also been linked to dry skin. Autoimmune disorders can present with skin conditions. Mast cell disorders can also be something to look for, with hives or redness.

2. **Bruising**: Another sign to evaluate is bruised skin. Do you suddenly have more bruises than usual? This could indicate anemia or an iron deficiency. Anemia can also cause fatigue, headaches, palpitations, and dizziness. Bruising can also be more present in those with vitamin C deficiencies. Bleeding disorders, medication, alcohol abuse and liver disease, and Vitamin K deficiency may be things to cross off the list if you can't correct easy bruising with diet and supplements.

3. **Palpitations**: Palpitations are your body's way of telling you that something is off. Whether it is stress, lack of sleep, stimulants (like coffee or nicotine), poor

diet, malnutrition, medication, electrolyte imbalances, vitamin and mineral deficiencies, or thyroid conditions—your body is trying to let you know. Of course as a reminder, always speak to your physician. These tips are just a starting point for your own health advocacy to get to know and understand your body and the signals it sends.

4. **How is your poop?** Constipation could indicate that you are not hydrated. It could indicate that you need to adjust your diet. The same goes for diarrhea, which can also indicate dehydration and the need to evaluate what you are eating. We all understand that our gut issues may be a chronic illness, so what I am specifically highlighting is that if you see anything outside of your normal, ask yourself what could your body be telling you? Sometimes an elimination diet can help determine if wheat, dairy, or other allergens are causing you troubles. Sometimes, it is just a matter of cleaning up what you eat. Do you eat more sugary snacks, processed foods, dyes, and preservatives than you do healthy, fresh food? I hate diet culture and there is no need to complicate anything or follow the diet trend of the year. Find balance, moderation, and learn what your body thrives off of, and also learn what your body doesn't like... then avoid that.

5. **Fatigue**: Some of us are no strangers to fatigue. For many of us in the chronic illness community, fatigue is part of our daily lives. However, it is important to understand your baseline in all of these categories, even pain and fatigue. Are you more fatigued than

usual? If so, that could point to low vitamin D or low iron. Fatigue could also indicate hypothyroidism. Your body is screaming that it is either overwhelmed with something it doesn't like, or lacking something it needs. It could be a sign of depression. Sometimes when you are depressed, getting out of bed feels like climbing Mount Everest. It could indicate a neurological issue or be a side effect of medication. It could also possibly indicate low blood pressure. Fatigue is definitely something to investigate.

6. **Headaches**: Headaches are caused by a number of things, but finding out what type of headache you have and what triggers it is an important skill to have in management. Hormone fluctuations can cause headaches, as well as poor hydration, poor sleep quality, hunger, stress, medication, and blood pressure issues. Sometimes a headache can be caused by ingredients that you may be sensitive to, whether it is something you ate or a fragrance you smell. Vitamin deficiencies, such as vitamin B, can cause headaches and migraines. POTS is a common and under-recognized condition that can also cause headaches. Finding the cause of your headache can help you to avoid triggers. If you can't figure out what causes your headaches, follow up with your healthcare provider.

These tips are not to stress you out or make you panic about everything that could go wrong. Take a deep breath. This is meant to help guide you with education about your body. Take notes and make a journal to document your health and mood. You may not realize a pattern until you go back and reread your health journal. You might even discover that your stomach ache has lasted for four months now. This is meant to make you mindful and to help yourself to advocate for your health.

You might realize that you need to stay hydrated and focus on better sleep. Maybe that means getting pain under control or changing your sleep routine. These tweaks and adjustments may relieve some of these common symptoms or signs. The body and mind need balance. We need rest, nutritious food, quality sleep, emotional support, and good hydration.

It is important to still follow up with your healthcare provider. During an annual checkup I was getting a regular breast exam. I always check for lumps and never noticed any. To my surprise, my physician found one. How had I missed that? Fortunately, after a biopsy, I discovered that the lump was benign. Even though I thought I knew my body, my physician was able to notice something I did not. If you are very in tune with yourself, you should still always keep regular appointments with your physician. This guide is not meant to replace professional help but to inspire you to know your body. You are the CEO of your body after all.

Advocating for Your Health

Though there are some amazing doctors in the world, there are also doctors who are not the best fit. You are entitled to a second or even third opinion. Because I am an invisible illness warrior, I have constantly needed to prove to healthcare providers that I knew something was wrong.

When I went in for skin cancer screening, I pointed out a spot on my face that was new. It was not like a typical funky mole that raises suspicion; instead, it looked like a skin tag. I joked around to my friends in our group chat, making them guess how many moles they would take. I am genetically prone to skin cancer but have always been in the clear, until recently. They sent me home with a clean bill of health and didn't even need to biopsy anything. Three months later, the skin tag grew and became red and painful, with a dry patch on top. Nothing was alleviating this spot. Being that it was on my face and making me self-conscious, I went back to the dermatologist.

"I know I'm crazy and was just here, but there is something wrong," I explained to the doctor as I pointed at my face. She insisted on taking a biopsy and said it looked suspicious. The results came back as squamous cell carcinoma, which is more aggressive than basal cell carcinoma. I can't help but wonder how much longer I would have left it if it weren't on my face, due to feeling like a crazy patient from previous years of medical gaslighting.

I have had to go back to follow up with the same issues after being dismissed at previous appointments, on many occasions. Here are a few ways to advocate for your health:

- **Bring a friend or loved one.** Sometimes having a second person can make a huge difference. They may be able to speak up for you if you feel like you can't. They may remember more of the appointment to recall if you were too nervous to retain everything. They are emotional support and can also help with accountability.

- **Take notes.** Appointments can be overwhelming, which can make it difficult to remember a lot of information. Taking notes will allow you to look back, whether it is later that day or months from now.
- **Come with a prepared list.** Having a list of medications, questions, and symptoms can help you to not leave out important details.
- **Ask for a copy.** Sometimes you can request a copy of your lab results to keep for your own records. If not, there is a medical records department who can provide you with copies, as it is your right as a patient. Personally, reading my reports has given me important health information that was left out.
- **Get another opinion.** You can see other doctors if you are not confident in the care you are receiving. It's just like dating… don't settle.
- **Find your voice.** Don't be afraid to speak up. How many times have you left an appointment and replayed the conversation based on what you wished you said? The doctor-patient relationship should be mutually respectful. You have a voice. Use it.
- **Find support groups.** I have always learned more from online support groups than my fifteen minute appointment with my doctor. Joining online support groups makes it easy to connect with others who have similar health issues. From health hacks to finding specialists, these groups can offer emotional and educational support from other patients.

Advocating for your health includes setting boundaries and advocating for your mental health as well as physical health. Life is far too short to waste your precious energy with people who do not respect you. If you are confident in your beliefs and values, protect them. Do not sway from who you are for the sake of appeasing someone else.

EIGHTEEN

Rewriting the Story

"Standin' on a hill in the mountain of dreams
Tellin' myself it's not as hard, hard, hard as it seems"
-Going to California by Led Zeppelin

Forgiveness is such a huge part of healing. When someone hurts you, it's like a thorn in your finger. You can choose to let it get inflamed or even infected and cause pain, or you can pull it out yourself, cleanse it and let it heal. Don't wait for an apology that you may never get. Relieve yourself from the anger and pain that someone gave you. When someone gives you something, that doesn't mean you need to keep it. Ask yourself if it is worth carrying around.

While being a single mom for a chunk of my life, I worked as a bartender for many years. The service industry is a great way to pile away instant cash and to pay last minute bills. I could have bills or rent due the next day and I could pick up a shift to keep myself afloat. The service industry is also a difficult environment with a rough lifestyle. Many people working in the industry are trying to get by. It could be a second or third job, they may be students, single mothers, in limbo between careers, or it's all they know. Many people I worked with had college degrees but the money was hard to leave for an entry level 9-5 career.

Things may be different now, but when I worked in restaurants, you sank or swam. You would get yelled at in the kitchen when everyone was in the weeds, people threw stuff, we joked around, we drank, and sexual harassment was just part of the everyday norm. When I was younger, I didn't have my voice yet and I didn't know how to be strong or speak up. Sinking wasn't an option, so I swam. The guys would twirl around a wet bar rag and use it as a whip, smacking my ass. I would have bruises that I'd notice later while in the shower. Several times I've had bruises in the shape of a handprint from getting my ass smacked. It was either cry and quit, or suck it up and play back. I had mouths to feed and bills to pay, so it was time to learn how to whip a bar rag back at the boys.

I remember when I was in my early twenties going to school during the weekdays to become a phlebotomist and EKG tech. I was a beer tub girl on the weekends and a hostess on weeknights at a restaurant. At the restaurant one night, it was slow and we were all sitting around. I was wearing ripped jeans and the owner stuck his finger in the rip of my pants, near my thigh. He looked at me, as if he was trying to read me and see how far he could go. It's interesting to look back and remember how powerless I felt and how much I have grown since. It is also important to remind myself that even though I know how to stick up for myself now, sometimes new experiences can be triggering and can leave a person feeling helpless.

REWRITING THE STORY

Not long ago, I was in the emergency room and the physician ordered an EKG. The medical assistant was young, maybe in his early twenties. Having a heart condition since birth, I have probably had a hundred EKGs. Typically the technician tries to be discreet and avoid exposing the patient's breasts. There are many ways to maneuver around without making the patient uncomfortable. Of course if the patient is not stable then it's speed over bedside manner. However, there I was, very alert and stable. I was just a chronic illness patient who was no stranger to the ER, getting a bag of fluids after an episode of dysautonomia. Suddenly, my breast was exposed for this young tech to see and everyone else around. He grabs my breast and holds it in his hand as he puts the leads on, saying he is covering me. I was so shocked that the woman I thought I was had just crumbled and couldn't even say a word. It had to be a mistake, I thought. Sure enough, he does this same thing to my other breast. He was fully grabbing my breast, holding it in his hand. I thought to myself, *this guy is straight up holding my naked breast right now. What the fuck? This can't be real.*

When I came home and processed everything, I told my husband and close friends, and I realized this was not okay. I felt guilty, like another man touched me, but I also didn't want to blow anything out of proportion. I was advised to say something to the hospital HR department. When I called, I was shocked at how seriously the hospital took everything. They made a police report, which I had to respond to, and told me this was assault. I instantly felt regretful and worried about ruining this young guy's life. I declined pressing charges. Because I was so used to having consequences for speaking up or standing up against sexual harassment, like getting fired or dismissed, I realized my brain was wired this way. I also spent years rewiring my brain to desensitize myself to what is appropriate and what is not.

I was amidst a transition from a time where sexual harassment was just a rite of passage to a #MeToo movement. I hope that my daughter never has to come home with hand-shaped bruises on her ass. I grew up in a time before cell phones and now raise my children, who have never known life without technology. My generation has seen the end of one era and the start of a new one. Together we are all trying to find our voices and to be heard. Over time I have seen each generation's baseline of what is acceptable or not, shift in a better direction.

Generational Patterns

What does home feel like to you? When I think of home, I think of warm and cozy. On a deeper level, what is home? When I was younger I fell in love with someone who "felt like home." Over the span of the next 10 years, he was in and out of my life. Sometimes, we were just friends who talked about photography, other times we were in love and even shared a home together. More often than not, we wouldn't even be on speaking terms. He felt like home. I associated that feeling with happiness. It wasn't until recently I realized that home for me back then was a nostalgic feeling. The Freudian complex of having a close connection with your parents, thus finding attraction to similar values, or dating people who resemble your mother/father, leads you to seek comfort in familiarity. He was, in fact, like my dad. The beard, light eyes, the music he listened to, cigarettes, his love for nature, and his brokenness matched with mine all resembled my dysfunctional home.

REWRITING THE STORY

Generational patterns continue because we continue to seek the familiarity of home. We seek friends and partners who share similar values. Our genes play a big role in what is passed onto us, but there is much more passed on besides DNA. Think about what you eat and your lifestyle. I have a friend who was raised by a woman who served her husband and family. Her mother made home-cooked meals and delivered their freshly folded laundry to their bedrooms. Now, she is that same wife and mother. There is nothing wrong with having roles in the home that fit the stereotypical gender roles, but this is another example of passing on patterns. Breaking those patterns means taking on the roles you want, not just because of what reproductive organs you have. It means putting aside your grandmother's meatloaf recipe and turning it into a keepsake. Instead of eating meals that were deemed healthy 40 years ago, find out what is deemed as healthy now. Are you continuing to eat a type of food because subconsciously it brings you back to that "home" feeling? Challenge yourself to eat new food and to create new recipes that maybe one day your children will cook for their children.

The next time you find yourself feeling a little stuck or lost, ask yourself if you are making choices based on what is familiar and comfortable. Sometimes leaping outside of your comfort zone can help to break up generational patterns. Try new food, date different types of people, and make new friends that are nothing like the ones you have now. Be open to diversity in every aspect of your life. Life as you know it is not the only truth.

Looking back at medical advances in my lifetime: I grew up in a time where I was told I would outgrow my illnesses, that I was just having growing pains, or that it was just stress. Though these are still stigmas that are here today, I see them lessen because of people in the chronic illness community sharing their stories. We are finding power in our voices and one day, hysteria will not be the go to diagnosis. We are on the brink of big changes.

Step Into Your Power

Sometimes being patient isn't always what it's cracked up to be. You can wait forever being anchored in the same spot, so choose wisely what you will allow to hold you back. Time always keeps moving ahead, whether you are ready or not. We always have reasons to be stagnant or fear change, as change is uncomfortable and not the easy route. Sometimes you need to let go and take the risk. I have let myself be held back far too many times in my life, due to allowing people to get in my way. Whether it is a relationship, friendship, business partner or family, if they are holding you back from your true potential, create some space and boundaries. We easily feel guilty for outgrowing others, so we let it hinder us.

It takes pain and frustration to ignite change. The best revolutions, movements, changes, and transformations stem from something that was negative. Use this as fuel to build something beautiful. You can let the storm tear you down or you can get up and find your purpose. Decide if you want to be a hostage in the battle or become a warrior because of it.

NINETEEN

Somewhere Over the Rainbow

"If you could
I know that you'd stay
We both know
Things don't work that way"
-Joanne by Lady Gaga

Check on your strong friends. As a strong friend, I appear stoic and put together. I am first to be there to offer a helping hand. I sense when you are not okay, even when you try to hide it. I will pull you out of the dark and carry you. Being a strong friend means that I am always there. Because I carry myself to be a warrior, most people assume I am fine and lean on me for support. Living with chronic illness, pain, and depression my entire life, I have learned how to face the world with something close to a smile every day.

When you live with a lifelong battle of depression and chronic pain, you master the disguise of appearing like you are doing well. I have always had major life changes, tragedies, and traumas in my life. I have never known an easy, stable, safe life. I have never known not scraping by, trying to stay afloat, or surviving. Nothing was ever handed to me. Nothing was ever

207

easy. Being in this position has usually led me to the role of being the strong friend. I always know what to do when the shit hits the fan. I am the MacGuyver of navigating through tragedy. I have even been told that my spirit animal is the elephant, because I am graceful and strong enough to carry others. There are so many times when I was not okay, but being the strong friend it was always assumed that I was. It was also the role I continued to play, further leading myself to struggle alone in solitude.

Our upbringing has taught us to keep our heads held high. When we continue to hide our pain, that pain inevitably grows into something more. The reality is, we can't always keep our heads up. It is okay to be angry. It is okay to cry. I can't tell you how many times I have been driving and a wave of grief hits. I have cried so many times in my car. I have unexpectedly burst into tears after taking a bite of food, worried I would choke. I have even done both... I have driven my car while eating a sandwich and crying. I can't imagine what any witnesses may have thought upon seeing such a mess.

Instead of numbing the pain, allow yourself to feel so that you can heal. I never realized how much I avoided feelings in my twenties, until I stopped drinking alcohol. Mental illness is often the gateway to addiction or alcohol abuse. When you constantly avoid working through pain and emotions, it will always follow you and resurface. It is difficult to feel the pain of a broken heart, but in order to manage it, you must process it and work through it.

I spent so many years numbing my pain, ignoring it, and dismissing the reality of my emotional state. Shortly after entering my thirties, I finally acknowledged my state of mind. I am forever grateful to have given up drinking alcohol when I lost my dad, so that I could grieve and work through it, rather than numb and worsen my emotions through alcohol.

SOMEWHERE OVER THE RAINBOW

I will never forget the look in my dad's eyes during his last few days. I was holding his hand, kneeling down next to his face as I touched his hair with my other hand and told him I loved him. With the little bit of strength he had left in his frail body, he opened his eyes wide open and lifted his face to mine. I could see the fear in his yellow eyes as he fought with everything he had to say something. No words came out, so I just kissed his forehead and told him everything was going to be okay. I had never seen him look so scared and it hurt to see him like that. I still wonder what was going on in his mind but I was able to comfort him, and that's all that matters.

I watched him over the years leading himself to this very moment and I couldn't do anything to stop it. I knew this would happen inevitably and I tried to prepare myself for years. The truth is nothing can prepare you for the heartbreak of a loved one crossing over. Heartache comes in waves and it never really goes away. Years later, a song, a scent, or a memory can knock you down as if it all just happened yesterday.

I spent the next year healing from the loss of my dad and getting to a more stable way of grieving. It is important to remember that we don't ever "get over it." Anyone who does not understand this is simply fortunate to not understand, because they have not experienced loss. We do not get over it, we just learn how to manage. The memories of my dad shifted from how he looked in the hospital to the younger and sober version of him. When I think about him now, I remember his sun kissed hair and when he was the best version of himself. I see his smile, not that look of fear. The pain was still there but I also experienced more feelings of gratitude than heartache.

GARDEN OF BLU

I went to Niagara Falls alone, to decompress after a brutal state of burnout from school and neglecting myself. I made the mistake of relapsing back into spreading myself too thin and not taking the much needed time for myself. I needed a reset. When I got to New York the weather was perfect. The few days felt like a dream and I was just within walking distance to the falls. I went each morning and again at night to take in the magic. There were flowers blooming everywhere. I was in awe of the cherry blossoms, tulips, and the forget-me-nots. I had not seen forget-me-not blooms, as we don't really see much of those in Florida. A few years prior, a few close friends of mine all got matching forget-me-not tattoos.

The day before I left, I saw two beautiful rainbows that were so close I felt like I could touch them. I have never been so close to a rainbow. I felt my dad's presence and gratitude for such a beautiful experience. I felt him and I felt at peace for the first time in awhile. The morning I was heading back home to Florida, I walked over to Niagara Falls one last time. It was 7:30 a.m. and in the same spot I had visited three other times, there was a rainbow. The rainbow was so close that I could almost touch it again. I felt a presence, though it was not like I had felt with my dad. I did not know what it meant, I just knew it was beautiful. I got to my car and turned it on. The radio was playing, Spirit in the Sky by Norman Greenbaum:

> "When I die and they lay me to rest
> Gonna go to the place that's the best
> When I lay me down to die
> Goin' up to the spirit in the sky"

I thought to myself, *"Wow, I hear you."*

SOMEWHERE OVER THE RAINBOW

I still didn't know who or what was sending me a sign, just that it was someone else, not my dad. It was someone who was sweet, soft, and beautiful. I felt grateful to have been sent such a beautiful hello.

As soon as I walked off the plane, I felt the humidity from the Florida heat. I knew I would miss the falls and the flowers. The dread of walking down the airport walkway to reality sank in. I had a new semester ready to begin, surgeries to schedule, and the never-ending break of being the busy woman that I am. I saw I had a call come in that only rang once. It was loud so I sent a text asking if everything was okay, gauging if the call was serious or just a random hello. "Not really," she said.

As I continued to find my way through the busy Orlando airport, I called back. "Someone killed her." I fell to the ground in the middle of the airport, hundreds of people walking around me as I tried to process this horrible news of one of my best friends. I felt as if my heart would stop. I couldn't find the words to give to console the very person who shares her DNA. In this moment, life would never be the same.

I finally made it to a healthier place of grieving the loss of my dad. I never thought I would ever hurt as much as I did then, only to find out that I could in fact hurt just as much, if not more. When you lose someone special in your life, it is so painful. When you lose someone who was in the prime of their life, glowing from the inside out, who was brutally taken from this world, there are no words to explain the pain. When you cry that hard, you have moments where you genuinely wonder if your heart is broken, that you too may die from such heartache. It is as if you can feel your heart breaking in half, or into a million pieces. There is no time limit on the grieving process. It is hard and you do not have to hurry up and be okay. The goal is to learn how to cope and manage the pain, and when to ask for help if needed.

In the beginning, gusts of grief would knock the wind out of me, like a cold, harsh reality wake up call. Suddenly I am hit hard and thinking to myself, *oh my God. It's real.*

No.

And just like that, I tell myself no, denying it is real until it sneaks up again. My soul could not believe it but my heart was racing as it knew the truth. I would allow my mind to skip over to a mundane thought that was easier to accept like, *did I check the mail?* Though denial is a normal part of grieving, we cannot deny it forever. Let it out. Scream if you must. Cry until your eyes swell shut and your voice breaks down. Release. Let the pain out. Grief is not linear. You will not simply stroll down a timeline and end at acceptance. One moment can take you right back to anger or denial. A song, a scent, a memory. It's okay. As much as it hurts, it is part of the process.

We feel grief the most when we are alone, not pretending to be strong in front of others; that's when we crumble. It's when the daunting tasks subside, the memorial is over, and everyone goes back to their normal lives. It hits you hard in those moments of solitude, when the silence of reality can't be shut out. I do feel that when we lose someone we love, a part of our hearts do break. They take that piece with them. Though we can slowly heal, that scar will always be there and sometimes it will hurt. But those who carry a piece of our hearts will always be with us as we are with them. They are our guardians now.

SOMEWHERE OVER THE RAINBOW

When a wave of mourning hits, it feels like waves crashing over me, heavily blanketing my body and violently dragging me under the water. Grief is a powerful wave. Some waves feel like a warm sinking feeling suddenly engulfing you, twisting your belly into knots. It grows up into your chest, grabbing ahold of your heart and ripping a piece off. Your throat tightens and you feel as if you'll suffocate from the pain. Your eyes fill, blurring the agony of the world around you. You will heal, but you'll be different now. Things will never be the same. Though a piece of you is missing, you gain an angel.

The presence of a loved one is woven into the fabric of your soul. They will always be there within you, even after they are gone. A human being is a tangible existence that we can comprehend. What we forget is people in our lives are woven in, even if just a thread. We don't visibly see or realize that everything that makes up who we are is connected to someone. We learn lessons in life, we get inspired, we pick up quirks, we adjust our perspective--not always on our own but from the influence of those who cross paths with us throughout our life. When a person leaves they leave their thread within the fabric of what makes you YOU. You are who you are because of something they contributed to your life, whether you realize it or not. They never really leave. And when they do leave, they would want you to be okay.

When a loved one leaves us, they become our guide or guardian. When you need them, call them. Close your eyes and ask them to hold your hand. Let them wipe away your tears when you are mournful. Let them celebrate you and cheer you on during moments of joy. As we face each dark storm, sometimes a rainbow appears. In many cultures, a rainbow symbolizes hope.

Rainbows motivate us to continue on during dark times. Our loved ones who pass will always be our rainbow. They will send messages if you look close enough. Honor the memory of your loved one in the way you live your life.

Close your eyes. Take a deep breath. Call your angel to wrap their love around you. Maybe they are holding your hand or maybe they are holding you. Feel only their love. You will always have this.

TWENTY

Some Flowers Bloom in the Dark

"We are the champions, my friends
And we'll keep on fighting till the end"
-We Are the Champions by Queen

I look back at younger versions of myself, like the one where I stood in church waiting for my prayers to be answered. This entire time, I now realize they were never answered. My heart never got better; in fact, it got worse. My dad never stopped drinking. Ultimately it is what killed him.

We can't control anything in life besides our own actions and perspective. My perspective is not the truth. No one's perspective is the truth. Everything thrown our way is processed and we all process things differently. If someone lived in my same shoes, living my same story, there would be different outcomes with a story told in a completely different perspective, ending in a completely different way. There is no right or wrong perspective. A bird's eye view will never be the same perspective as that of an ant.

GARDEN OF BLU

As often as you may feel out of control in life, you still have the power to steer back into the desired direction or even go somewhere new. If you get lost, sometimes you just need to see where you end up; it may be better than where you were headed. The unknown can be scary but it can also take you somewhere beautiful. No matter what, experiences in life mean that you are trying, learning, and growing. Grow through it all until you blossom, then grow some more.

I am not sure why I always had such a deeply low self-worth. It's not like my parents didn't tell me they loved me enough. Sometimes I wonder if it was because I was such a late bloomer and when all of the boys started to check out the girls, I was exempt. Maybe we are all just trying to recover from our childhood. Through the eyes of an adult, none of it seems like a big deal until later we are the adults looking back to a time in which we started to build our brick walls.

Our insecurities can turn us into monsters if we let them take over. And since misery loves company, when somebody close to you starts to find a little light while you constantly sit in the dark together, you tend to dim their light a little because you don't want to be left there alone. Pay closer attention. If you start to feel salty when you see a friend finding success or growing in a way in which you haven't yet, set those thoughts on fire. If you can't be a cheerleader then maybe you need to question whether or not you are happy, and how you can also elevate, rather than trying to anchor them back down. It is hard enough when most of us hold ourselves back, but when the people you think love and care about you also hold you back, it can be devastating.

Don't ever not be genuine. Always have authenticity and transparency. Don't ever fake anything. If you truly can't find it in yourself to be happy for others then it's time to do some soul-searching and reflecting and ask yourself why not? It is time to stop spilling the tea and start filling up other people's cups. Life is too short to dwell on petty things.

I used to hate myself. People could see right through me and knew that I had no self-worth. I have been taken advantage of because of that. I have wandered aimlessly and lost throughout most of my life. Once I entered my thirties, I finally acknowledged my brokenness. I slowly dug deeper and picked up the pieces, mending some and creating some new ones. Pain is pain, and trauma is trauma; however, I appreciate the beauty of what grows from the dirt. I am thankful that I did not have my life mapped out for me to skip through as I stop and smell each rose. Instead, I got to appreciate beauty even more. I got to rebuild a new foundation into whatever I wanted, rather than what was built for me. I look back at the child within myself, the broken girl I once was, and I hold her. I still have so much more growth ahead of me. I let go of the past to let my fire blaze a new way.

Some flowers bloom in the dark. When thinking about growth, think about a seed. In order for a seedling to sprout, the shell must first crack and fall apart. A seed will split apart, breaking and appearing destroyed. Then, there is growth and blooming. When we grow, it looks and feels like we are falling apart. When you find yourself feeling broken, just know that you are about to bloom. Just because you cannot see the light at the end of the tunnel does not mean it is not there. The ebbs and flows in life show us that one moment can turn everything around and easily crumble. There will always be things that don't make sense when times are tough. Hold on to the good, the beauty, the lessons, the growth, and the light.

Healing is not instant gratification. It is an ongoing journey. You can overcome your darkness and rise from the flames like a phoenix, as your ashes from the past fall beneath you. After each fall, resurrection and rebirth may follow. Get your ass up and transform.

AFTERWORD
Christine Gosch-Echevarria, M.D.

Misti Blu Day is a blossoming rosebud in my life, as well as for so many others. She keeps me grounded, gives me so much perspective in all aspects of life and I am so amazed at her wealth of knowledge and growth.

I met Misti 4 years ago. She is my husband's niece from his first marriage. Misti came to visit us in Missouri, shortly after my husband's first divorce and we had just met. She has always amazed and inspired me. She treated me like family from the first day I met her. She's kind, caring, so charismatic, so brilliant and so multi-talented. She reminds me of a beautiful rose that's just about to open – so bright and resilient, beauty glowing from around her, but with so much underneath her outside petals, as well as such elegance still yet to express itself. In the few years I have known her, I have learned some of her history and have spent some time talking to her about her health conditions, as I am a physician and it intrigues me, and also gives me a sense of meaning to maybe offer some inside help to her. After reading her book, there's so much more behind the scenes that no one could imagine. I feel so honored to have been asked to write the afterword for her book. I have learned so much about Misti, as well as about myself, from reading her book.

Misti is an advocate for herself as well as anyone who will allow her to help them. She's 20 years younger than me, but I feel she is so much wiser in so many of the things that really matter in life – the things that make our existence pleasurable and sustainable. She has truly risen and triumphed from a place that most are not able to recover from. Recovery is an everyday, all day, all life thing. Life is what we make it. It's so easy to find ourselves falling into a place of doom and gloom, feeling desperate or having self-pity. In her book, Misti teaches us to use the bad things to teach us that there are good things that complement the bad. She teaches us to let go of what doesn't serve us. If someone is "bad" for us, don't waste energy or time on them. This is such an important concept. We are who we hang out with. Our perspective is so influenced by the energy of those around us, as is the opposite! We can make such an impact on others by just changing our perspective as well. Look for the bright and positive things.

Living with chronic health problems can be emotionally and physically exhausting. A person feels so unheard and alone. One often even questions their own sanity while going through the workup and diagnosis process. It can take multiple physicians and many years to get the right answers and then sometimes, those aren't answers we want to hear. A person who has chronic illnesses has to learn to be their own cheerleader, their own therapist, their own recharger - they have to be able to stay strong and pick themselves back up when they fall down, so that their life doesn't get them down. It's not unusual even for medical professionals to challenge the sanity of someone with difficult to diagnose, unclear subtle diseases. Misti has shown us how to get through this struggle, come to terms with answers she might not like to hear, stay strong, live a happy life and continue to prosper.

Misti, to me, is that perfect rosebud, just starting to open, already so beautiful and has so much to offer the world, but wait! She's just opening up! Wait until her petals are in full bloom! Wait until she flourishes and spreads her love and wealth of knowledge and experience to help others. There are a few thorns that she keeps so well hidden because they are just there to protect her from the useless damage of others. She's so radiant and shines everywhere she goes. I can't wait for what she has to offer the world next. I feel very blessed to have Misti in my life and to watch her open her petals fully. She's a rosebud that will never wilt, never turn dusky, never dry up, never fall over. Her edges might tatter ever so slightly, but they will fluff right back up and be in full bloom before you can blink. Bloom away Misti Blu Day! We love you!

The National Suicide
Prevention Lifeline is
1-800-273-8255

Made in the USA
Middletown, DE
18 August 2021

46319823R00132